Exploring the American Presidency through 50 Historic Treasures

AMERICAN ASSOCIATION *for* STATE *and* LOCAL HISTORY

Exploring America's Historic Treasures

SERIES EDITOR
Rebecca K. Shrum, Indiana University-Purdue University Indianapolis

MANAGING EDITOR
Aja Bain, AASLH

About the Organization
The American Association for State and Local History (AASLH) is a national history membership association headquartered in Nashville, Tennessee, that provides leadership and support for its members who preserve and interpret state and local history in order to make the past more meaningful to all people. AASLH members are leaders in preserving, researching, and interpreting traces of the American past to connect the people, thoughts, and events of yesterday with the creative memories and abiding concerns of people, communities, and our nation today. In addition to sponsorship of this book series, AASLH publishes the *History News* magazine, a newsletter, technical leaflets and reports, and other materials; confers prizes and awards in recognition of outstanding achievement in the field; supports a broad education program and other activities designed to help members work more effectively; and advocates on behalf of the discipline of history. To join AASLH, go to www.aaslh.org or contact Membership Services, AASLH, 2021 21st Ave. South, Suite 320, Nashville, TN 37212.

About the Series
The American Association for State and Local History publishes the Exploring America's Historic Treasures series to bring to life topics and themes from American history through objects from museums and other history organizations. Produced with full-color photographs of historic objects, books in this series investigate the past through the interpretation of material culture.

Exploring the American Presidency through 50 Historic Treasures

KIMBERLY A. KENNEY

ROWMAN & LITTLEFIELD
Lanham • Boulder • New York • London

Published by Rowman & Littlefield
An imprint of The Rowman & Littlefield Publishing Group, Inc.
4501 Forbes Boulevard, Suite 200, Lanham, Maryland 20706
www.rowman.com

86-90 Paul Street, London EC2A 4NE

British Library Cataloguing in Publication Information Available

Library of Congress Cataloging-in-Publication Data

ISBN: 978-1-5381-5663-6 (cloth : alk. paper)
ISBN: 978-1-5381-5664-3 (electronic)

∞™ The paper used in this publication meets the minimum requirements of
American National Standard for Information Sciences—Permanence of Paper
for Printed Library Materials, ANSI/NISO Z39.48-1992.

Contents

Acknowledgments

This book would not have been possible without the assistance of my colleagues at presidential sites across the country. I reached out to them to select an artifact that best represented their president. It was no small task to narrow it down to just one! After more than 20 years at the McKinley Presidential Library & Museum, I know it was a difficult decision for me. It has been a lot of fun getting to know the other presidents through the objects they used during their lifetimes.

I would like to thank the following individuals for their help in not only selecting an artifact, but also sharing its unique story with me so that I could write this book: Down Bonner and Mary V. Thompson, George Washington's Mount Vernon; Kelly P. Cobble, Adams National Historic Park; Gardiner Hallock, Thomas Jefferson's Monticello; Elizabeth Chew and Hilarie M. Hicks, James Madison's Montpelier; Jarod Kearney, James Monroe Museum and Memorial Library; Marsha Mullin, The Hermitage; Mike Wasko, Martin Van Buren National Historic Site; Roger Hardig, Benjamin Harrison Presidential Site; Annique Dunning, Sherwood Forest Plantation Foundation; Rachel Helvering and Candice Roland Candeto, President James K. Polk Home & Museum; Rachelle Moyer Francis, Millard Fillmore House; Patrick Clarke, President James Buchanan's Wheatland, LancasterHistory; Jim Orr, The Henry Ford; Melissa Trombley-Prosch, Ulysses S. Grant Cottage National Historic Landmark; Gil Gonzalez and Julie Mayle, Rutherford B. Hayes Presidential Library & Museums; Todd Arrington, James A. Garfield National Historic Site; Sharon Farrell, Grover Cleveland Birthplace New Jersey Historic Site; Cade Martin, photographer; Ruth Horstman, William Howard Taft National Historic Site; Andrew Phillips, Woodrow Wilson Presidential Library; Sherry Hall, Warren G. Harding Presidential Sites; Julie Bartlett Nelson, Calvin Coolidge Presidential Library & Museum; William Jenney, President Coolidge State Historic Site; Marcus E. Eckhardt, Herbert Hoover Presidential Library-Museum; Michelle Frauenburger, Franklin D. Roosevelt Presidential Library and Museum; Clay Bauske, Harry S. Truman Presidential Library and Museum; Dawn Hammat and William Snyder, Dwight D. Eisenhower Presidential Library, Museum, and Boyhood Home; John F. Kennedy Presidential Library and Museum; Renée Gravois Bair, Lyndon B. Johnson Presidential Library and Museum; Christine Mickey, Richard Nixon Presidential Library and Museum; Donald Halloway, Brooke Clement, Noelle Ward, and Joel Westphal, Gerald R. Ford Presidential Library & Museum; Meredith Evans and Timothy Rives, Jimmy Carter Presidential Library and Museum; Duke Blackwood and Steve Branch, Ronald Reagan Presidential Library and Museum; Jay Patton, George H. W. Bush Presidential Library and Museum; Jennifer Wisniewski, William J. Clinton Presidential Library and Museum; Kelly Seufert, George W. Bush Presidential Library and Museum; Steven Booth, Barack Obama Presidential Library; Phil Rokus, Office of the Senate Curator; Alexandra Lane, White House Historical Association, and Robert J. Baruda, National Museum of the United States Air Force.

This is the ninth book I've published, and I always use this space to thank my amazing family for their support in all of my endeavors: my grandmother Marjorie Vanderhoof, my mother Cheryl Beach, and my sister Kristen Merrill. I know I've said it before, but you truly are the best team of cheerleaders anyone could ask for! And finally, thank you to my wife, Karen Everman, for her unwavering support of this project. She was a marvelous copy editor, and her curiosity made this book even better. She inspires me every single day.

Timeline of Objects

If a specific date is known for the object itself, it has been noted.

1841
William Henry Harrison
Flag Remnant (1811), page 33

1841–1845
John Tyler
Piano (1841), page 36

1845–1849
James K. Polk
Table, page 38

1849–1850
Zachary Taylor
Chair (1847), page 41

1850–1853
Millard Fillmore
Engraving of Debate (1855), page 44

1853–1857
Franklin Pierce
Kansas-Nebraska Act (1854), page 47

1857–1861
James Buchanan
Law Books, page 51

1861–1865
Abraham Lincoln
Chair from Ford's Theatre (1865), page 54

1865–1869
Andrew Johnson
Impeachment Note (1868), page 59

1869–1877
Ulysses S. Grant
Inkwell, page 62

1877–1881
Rutherford B. Hayes
Morgan Silver Dollar (1878), page 64

1880
Resolute Desk, page 154

1881
James A. Garfield
Inaugural Address (1881), page 67

1881–1885
Chester Arthur
Tiffany Screen (1883), page 71

1885–1889 and 1893–1897
Grover Cleveland
Ribbon from Naval Review (1893),
page 74

1889–1893
Benjamin Harrison
Judge Cartoon (1889), page 77

1897–1901
William McKinley
Bank (1901–1905), page 81

1901–1909
Theodore Roosevelt
Page from Speech (1912), page 87

1909–1913
William Howard Taft
Bible, page 89

1913–1921
Woodrow Wilson
1919 Pierce-Arrow, page 92

1921–1923
Warren G. Harding
Skeleton Key, page 96

1923–1929
Calvin Coolidge
Painting of Inauguration (1923), page 98

1929–1933
Herbert Hoover
Humidor (1933), page 101

1933–1945
Franklin D. Roosevelt
Fireside Chat Microphone, page 105

1945–1953
Harry S. Truman
"The Buck Stops Here" Desk Sign
(1945), page 111

1945
First airplane used to transport the president. It was a Douglas VC-54C Skymaster, known unofficially as the "Sacred Cow," page 170

1945
Presidential Seal was standardized, page 157

1953–1961
Dwight D. Eisenhower
Globe, page 114

1961–1963
John F. Kenney
PT 109 Coconut Husk (1943), page 117

1963–1969
Lyndon B. Johnson
Desk Blotter (1969), page 120

1965
White House Historical Association
begins collecting presidential
portraits, page 163

1969–1974
Richard Nixon
Easy Chair, page 123

1969
Senate Ballot Box used for Electoral
College votes. Similar boxes have been
used since 1877. The Electoral College
was established in the US Constitution,
which was signed in 1787, page 166

1974–1977
Gerald Ford
Statuette of Elephant and Donkey,
page 127

1977–1981
Jimmy Carter
Hungarian Crown (1998),
page 129

1981–1989
Ronald Reagan
Piece of the Berlin Wall (1961), page 132

1989–1993
George H. W. Bush
Letter to Family (1990), page 135

1993–2001
Bill Clinton
Saxophone (1994), page 138

2001–2009
George W. Bush
Bullhorn (2001), page 141

2009–2017
Barack Obama
Pen Used to Sign Affordable Care Act
(2010), page 145

2017–2021
Donald Trump
MAGA Hat (2018), page 148

2021–
Joe Biden
COVID-19 Vaccine Vial (2021), page 151

Introduction

Artifacts have a unique power to convey the immediacy of history. Unlike documents, artifacts represent the raw, uninterpreted story of our past. The study of objects is called material culture, and learning how to "read" objects is an important component of museum studies training. Material culture is a fascinating lens through which we tell stories all the time in museums, but the average person does not often consider the power of objects. The "50 Historic Treasures" series is closing that gap by highlighting objects as the tradition bearers of our national story.

American presidents are often seen as larger than life, especially the ones who were assassinated or otherwise died in office. By exploring these men through the everyday objects that tell their stories, they become more relevant as we look at them as human beings. The objects they used during their presidencies are often ordinary items that became extraordinary because of their association with a famous person. But the objects themselves are all relatable.

Can you imagine trying to eat if you had George Washington's teeth in your mouth? What objects are symbolic of your own friendships, like the walking stick Thomas Jefferson's family presented to James Madison? Can you picture the horror of the tragic scene in the President's Box at Ford's Theatre when the chair Abraham Lincoln was sitting in was suddenly covered in his blood? Did John F. Kennedy relive his dramatic survival every time he looked at the PT 109 coconut husk that was fashioned into a paperweight on his Oval Office desk? Where were you when George W. Bush climbed a pile of rubble at Ground Zero a few days after 9/11 and spoke to the crowd using that now famous bullhorn? Using objects to explore the American presidency is perhaps the most powerful way that we can illustrate and demonstrate the relevance of history.

Most of the artifacts included in this book were chosen by the very people who have been charged with stewarding the legacies of the relatively small number of men who have held the highest office in the land. Through their expertise, insight, and guidance, I was able to write about objects that they felt best represented their president. My correspondence with museum staff gave me access to unique stories that are not necessarily available to the general public.

One note about the number of chapters in this book: Grover Cleveland, our 22nd and 24th president, is the only person to serve two nonconsecutive terms. This means that while Joe Biden is our 46th president, he is only the 45th person elected president. I have selected five iconic artifacts that represent the presidency more broadly to round out the 50 historic treasures: the Resolute desk, presidential seal, official presidential portraits, the Senate ballot box for the Electoral College votes, and Air Force One.

I hope you enjoy this unique trip through presidential history!

1

George Washington, 1789–1797: Dentures

No figure in American history is revered more than George Washington. Like many American presidents, he has been placed high upon a pedestal as a war hero and founding father, which makes it difficult to relate to him. But there is one artifact at Mount Vernon that speaks to his humanity: his dentures.

Everyone has experienced a toothache from time to time, and although most of us do not suffer as much as Washington did, the fact that he endured this common condition makes him more relevant and relatable to modern sensibilities. He was often in pain, likely while he was commanding troops during the Revolutionary War and laying the foundation for our first government as an independent nation.

Washington's dental problems began in his 20s and plagued him his entire life. Historians speculate that the likely culprits were a combination of disease, genetics, and a poor diet, which was common in the 18th century. When he was 24, Washington noted in his diary that he paid a doctor to remove one of his teeth. His writings often mention sore teeth, aching gums, and ill-fitting dentures, and his ledgers reveal a variety of dental-related purchases, including toothbrushes, dental cleansers, and pain medication.[1] Before the Revolution, Dr. John Baker created a partial set of teeth for Washington using ivory that was attached to his remaining teeth with wire. In the 1780s, Dr. Jean-Pierre Le Mayeur also tried to help Washington, although no records survive of those services. In his advertisements, Dr. Mayeur said he specialized in "transplanting" real teeth, but there is no evidence to suggest that he tried this

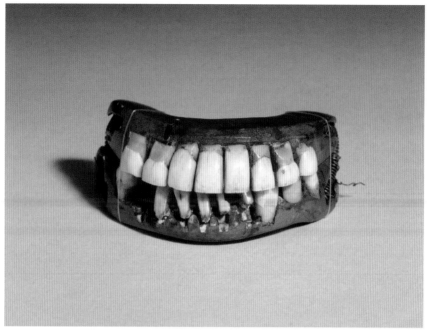

Contrary to popular legend, George Washington's dentures were not made of wood. They were made from human teeth.
GEORGE WASHINGTON'S MOUNT VERNON

procedure on Washington. It is likely that Dr. Mayeur created a bigger set of false teeth for Washington as his remaining teeth failed. By his inauguration in 1789, Washington had only one of his own teeth left in his mouth.[2]

Washington's first set of false teeth as president were made with the latest advances available at the time. According to Mount Vernon, "Dr. John Greenwood—a New York dentist, former soldier in the Revolution, and a true pioneer in American dentistry—fashioned a technologically advanced set of dentures carved out of hippopotamus ivory and employing gold wire springs and brass screws holding human teeth. Greenwood even left a hole in the dentures to accommodate Washington's single tooth as he believed a dentist should 'never extract a tooth . . . [when] there is a possibility of saving it.' When Washington finally lost this tooth as well, he gave it to Greenwood who saved this cherished item in a special case."[3] Today that case is preserved in the collection of the New York Academy of Medicine, with an inscription that it was removed in 1790, after Washington became president.[4]

Washington would have several pairs of dentures made for him, but all of them were ill fitting and painful. It was difficult for him to eat or talk, and they actually changed the way he looked. George Washington Parke Custis noted "a marked change . . . in the appearance . . . more especially in the projection of the under lip." This disfigurement is evident in the famous 1796 painting by Gilbert Stuart. Even the high-end dentures made by Dr. Greenwood gave him no relief. Washington complained that they were "both uneasy in the mouth and bulge my lips out" and that the teeth "have, by degrees, worked loose."[5]

Over time, we have come to believe the popular myth of "George Washington's wooden teeth," when in fact most of his dentures, including the only full set to survive in Mount Vernon's collection, were made of human teeth, some of which were likely purchased from enslaved people who did not have a choice in the matter. On May 8, 1784, George Washington noted in his ledger that he paid 6 pounds 2 shillings to "Negroes for 9 Teeth, on acc[oun]t of the French Dentis[t] Doct[o]r Lemay."[6] The fate of those teeth is not documented, as Mount Vernon explains: "Whether the teeth provided by the Mount Vernon enslaved people were simply being sold to the dentist for any patient who needed them or intended for George Washington, is unknown. Since Washington paid for the teeth it suggests that they were either for his own use or for someone in his family. It is important to note that while Washington paid these enslaved people for their teeth it does not mean they had a real option to refuse his request."[7]

Many people today are unaware or uncomfortable with the fact that Washington was an enslaver. He was born on a tobacco plantation in Virginia on February 22, 1732, to a slave-owner. Through his first occupation as a surveyor, Washington became interested in purchasing his own land. He inherited his father's plantation and added to his wealth exponentially when he married Martha Dandridge Custis in 1759.[8] Washington had inherited 10 enslaved people from his father when he was still a child, and later purchased 8 more himself, but his wife came to the Union with 84 enslaved people, making her one of the richest women in Virginia. Recent publications, such as *Never Caught: The Washingtons' Relentless Pursuit of Their Runaway Slave, Ona Judge* by Erica Armstrong Dunbar, have examined Washington more closely through the lens of slavery. The History Channel has also explored his complicated relationship with those he held in bondage:

> By the standards of his day, Washington treated his enslaved workers better than most. But he expected more from them than the average slave, especially as he

began to use his plantation as a kind of efficiency experiment. The future president tried out new farming techniques, closely monitored his enslaved workers' production in connection with the farm's yield. He whipped, beat, and separated people from their families as punishment. Washington also relentlessly pursued escaped slaves and circumvented laws that would allow his enslaved workers freedom if they did manage to escape to neighboring states.[9]

As Washington grew older, his views on slavery began to change. Toward the end of his life he wrote, "The unfortunate condition of the persons, whose labour in part I employed, has been the only unavoidable subject of regret. To make the Adults among them as easy & as comfortable in their circumstances as their actual state of ignorance & improvidence would admit; & to lay a foundation to prepare the rising generation for a destiny different from that in which they were born; afforded some satisfaction to my mind, & could not I hoped be displeasing to the justice of the Creator."[10] In his will, Washington recorded his desire that his enslaved people be set free after his wife's death.

So why does the myth of "George Washington's wooden teeth" persist? The most common explanation is that the ivory used in some of his dentures likely became stained over time, and perhaps resembled a wood grain to the casual observer. There are references to "wooden teeth" in historical publications as late as the mid-20th century. The truth is, there were far more advanced methods of constructing dentures in Washington's time, and although he never got the relief he was looking for, he was able to obtain the best dentures, made with the latest technological advances.

John Adams, 1797–1801: Law Desk

As the successor to larger-than-life George Washington, John Adams narrowly won the election of 1796 against his friend and political opponent Thomas Jefferson. He had been dissatisfied in his role as the nation's first vice president under Washington, complaining that it was "the most insignificant office that ever the invention of man contrived or his imagination conceived."[1] In his article "John Adams: Campaigns and Elections," C. James Taylor suggests that Adams saw himself as the "heir apparent" under Washington, which may have been the only reason he endured eight years as vice president.[2]

Adams seemed better suited to the more active roles he had played earlier in his life as a founding father, including being elected to the Massachusetts Assembly, representing his colony at the First Continental Congress, and serving on over 90 committees that would guide the creation of a new government. It was Adams who chose George Washington to lead the Continental Army in the Revolutionary War, and it was his idea that each colony should maintain its own independent government.

Prior to entering a life of public service, Adams studied law at Harvard University, which prepared him well for a career in politics. One artifact that captures all of his roles as a lawyer, vice president, and president is his law desk in the collection of the Adams National Historic Park in Quincy, Massachusetts. It depicts the busy life of a politician, with labeled compartments for his papers:

No. 1 Sundry letters & reports from Sec. of State

No. 2 - - - - from Sec of War & Navy

No. 3 - - - - from Sec of Treasury

No. 4 - - - - from Attorney General

No. 5 Reports of the Heads of dep on the following subjects

The powers & duties of the Account at War

Answers to questions proposed by the President

Proper measures to be recommended at the opening of the several sessions of Congress on

1797 '90.99.1000.

No. 6 Draughts of Speeches

No. 7 Papers related to the rank of Gen Knox & Hamilton[3]

John Adams used this desk as a lawyer, vice president, and president.

NATIONAL PARK SERVICE, ADAMS NATIONAL HISTORICAL PARK

As a lawyer, Adams's belief in "a government of laws, and not of men" justified taking on unpopular cases, a trait he carried through to his presidency. For example, he defended the British soldiers who fired on the colonists in what became known as the Boston Massacre, in spite of his role as a leader against colonial rule. Of the eight soldiers tried, six were acquitted and two were found guilty of the lesser charge of manslaughter. Later he would record his thoughts in his diary, recalling the case as "one of the best pieces of service I ever rendered my country. Judgment of death against those soldiers would have been as foul a stain upon this country as the executions of the Quakers or witches."[4]

Frequently described as a workaholic, Adams was "abrasive and thin skinned" such that he was often difficult to get along with.[5] During the 1796 election, newspapers of the day accused him of being an Anglophile who was "secretly bent on establishing a family dynasty by having his son succeed him as president."[6] Indeed, when his son John Quincy Adams was elected president in 1824, John Adams would become the first father of a president who had also served in the office himself.

The policies Adams supported were rooted in what he thought was right, not political expediency, which ultimately cost him reelection. His support of legislation such as the Naturalization Act, the Alien Enemies Act, and the Sedition Act,[7] created a hotly contested election in the fall of 1800 that would ultimately split the Federalist Party and pave the way for Jefferson to win. Nasty political campaigns are not unique to the 21st century. In fact, some of the insults and outright lies spun in 18th- and 19th-century campaigns rival tabloids in the modern age, as Taylor explains:

> The level of personal attack by both parties knew no bounds. At one point, Adams was accused of plotting to have his son marry one of the daughters of King George III and thus establish a dynasty to unite Britain and the United States. The plot had been stopped, according to the story, only by the intervention of George Washington, who had dressed in his old Revolutionary War uniform to confront Adams with sword in hand. Jefferson, meanwhile, was accused of vivisection and of conducting bizarre ritualistic rites at Monticello, his home in Virginia.[8]

Political rival Alexander Hamilton published his own reasons for not supporting Adams, saying he was "emotionally unstable, given to impulsive and irrational decisions, unable to coexist with his closest advisors, and generally unfit to be President."[9]

In the end, Jefferson received 73 electoral votes and 65 went to Adams, who left Washington to return to his family farm in Massachusetts. He led a relatively quiet life there, spending most of his time writing correspondence and his autobiography, quite possibly at the very desk he had used throughout his professional life to create policies and organize his papers. According to Taylor, "Nothing seemed too trivial or too weighty for him to address, from the nature of his manure piles at the farm to history and political philosophy."[10]

Adams died on July 4, 1826, the same day as Thomas Jefferson, on the 50th anniversary of America's independence. His desk is now on display at the Adams National Historic Site, which is comprised of the two oldest presidential birth sites in the country: The Old House at Peacefield, the home of four generations of the Adams family, and the Stone Library, which was constructed by Charles Francis Adams to house his father's and grandfather's vast collection of books.

Thomas Jefferson, 1801–1809: Great Clock at Monticello

The mansion at Monticello is widely regarded as Thomas Jefferson's finest masterpiece, perhaps second only to the Declaration of Independence itself, which he helped write. Eventually encompassing 11,000 square feet, Jefferson designed the house himself in 1769. After returning from France, he oversaw its renovation and expansion between 1796 and 1809.

The Great Clock, also designed by Jefferson, enjoys a prominent spot in the home with one face in the Entrance Hall and another face on the exterior on the east side. According to the Thomas Jefferson Foundation, "With its dual faces and hour-striking gong, the Great Clock at Monticello served the residents of the house as well as the workers in the field. Its design evinces Jefferson's desire for order, which he exerted over his family and the enslaved community at Monticello. It also reveals his love of innovation and his ability to modify the traditional to suit his needs. It was as much a topic of conversation in Jefferson's time as it remains today."[1]

The Great Clock was built from Jefferson's design by Peter Spurck of Philadelphia between 1792 and 1793 and installed at Monticello from 1804 to 1805. It has many unique features, including the absence of a minute hand on the exterior clock face, the use of IIII to indicate the number 4 instead of IV, and a day of the week indicator marked by the position of the clock's weights along the wall. In her book *The Worlds of Jefferson at Monticello*, Susan Stein writes, "The lack of a minute-hand is not a clockmaker's mistake but part of Jefferson's design. Because of the size of the face and the markings between the hour figures, the hour-hand itself would do the work of the minute-hand. The figure IIII is used on the clockface rather than IV. There are several reasons behind this. First, it provides a better visual balance on the clock face. Second, IIII is actually how the Romans wrote 4. The practice of using the subtractive forms of IV for 4 and IX for 9, etc. did not develop until about 1300 A.D."[2] The interior clock face has both a minute hand on the large dial and a small dial that counts seconds. According to Monticello, "The clock was wound every Sunday with a cranklike key, and a folding ladder was made in the Monticello joinery for that task."[3] Today the clock is still wound each Sunday morning by a member of the staff.

While working on his design in 1792, Jefferson wrote to Henry Remsen, who worked for the state department at the foreign desk, to ask about a specific component of his clock. "The Chinese have a thing made of a kind of bell metal, which they call a Gong, and is used as a bell at the gates of large houses &c.," he wrote. "I wish for one to serve as the bell to a clock, which might be heard all over my farm."[4]

The clock was finished in 1793, but Jefferson was not happy with Spurck's workmanship. In a letter to Robert Leslie, to whom Spurck was apprenticed, Jefferson said, "My large clock could not be made to go by Spurck. I ascribed it to the bungling manner in which he had made it. I was obliged to let him make the striking movement anew on the common plan, after which it went pretty well."[5] Historians believe the clock was originally installed in Jefferson's Philadelphia home before being moved to Monticello when he returned to Virginia in 1794. It was at this time that Jefferson also found a gong to complete his vision for his Great Clock, which was loud enough to be heard across his five-thousand-acre plantation.

While he was president, Jefferson ordered the weights for his clock in 1804 from the Foxall Foundry in Washington, D.C. He soon realized that the length of the weights that measured the days of the week was greater than the height of the Entrance Hall. His solution was to cut a hole in floor, just big enough for each of the six 18-pound cannonball weights to pass through, where his calendar continues with "Saturday" written on the cellar wall.

The lives of the enslaved people at Monticello would have been strictly governed by the sound of this clock marking the hours of the day. Although he owned more than six hundred people during his lifetime, making him one of the largest slaveholders in Virginia, Jefferson's relationship to the institution of slavery is complicated. His political views were not always in step with his actions. For example, he included a section in his original version of the Declaration of Independence that criticized the slave trade, but it was ulti-

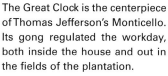

The Great Clock is the centerpiece of Thomas Jefferson's Monticello. Its gong regulated the workday, both inside the house and out in the fields of the plantation.
THOMAS JEFFERSON FOUNDATION AT MONTICELLO

mately removed by Congress before the final draft. During his presidency, the international slave trade was banned, and early in his political career he had attempted to have slavery banned in the Western Territories.[6] According to Monticello, "Throughout his entire life, Thomas Jefferson was publicly a consistent opponent of slavery. Calling it a 'moral depravity' and a 'hideous blot,' he believed that slavery presented the greatest threat to the survival of the new American nation. Jefferson also thought that slavery was contrary to the laws of nature, which decreed that everyone had a right to personal liberty. These views were radical in a world where unfree labor was the norm."[7]

And yet, scientific evidence proves that he had a long-term relationship with Sally Hemings, an enslaved person on his plantation, and fathered four of her children. He emancipated two of his children with Hemings, but the other two remained enslaved during his lifetime, only receiving their freedom in his will. Jefferson never freed Hemings herself. It was his daughter Martha who granted her freedom after Jefferson's death. It is difficult to reconcile that a man who advocated for the abolition of slavery only enslaved people himself, but owned his own children, which was actually not uncommon. Enslaved women were not able to stop the sexual advances of their owners, which led to many children of mixed race in Virginia and throughout the South. Children born to enslaved women were automatically enslaved themselves.

The exact nature of Hemings and Jefferson's relationship will never be known. The historical record simply does not contain enough information. What historians do know is that Hemings traveled to Paris with Jefferson's daughter Maria while he was serving as ambassador to France. According to Monticello, "Unlike countless enslaved women, Sally Hemings was able to negotiate with her owner. In Paris, where she was free, the 16-year-old agreed to return to enslavement at Monticello in exchange for 'extraordinary privileges' for herself and freedom for her unborn children. Over the next 32 years Hemings raised four children—Beverly, Harriet, Madison, and Eston—and prepared them for their eventual emancipation."[8] Sally's son Madison described his mother as Jefferson's "concubine," noting that she initially refused to return to America with him. Only after she negotiated these "privileges" did she agree to accompany him back to Virginia. It is not known why Hemings trusted Jefferson to keep his promises to her, or if she tried to negotiate her own freedom.

Jefferson believed in the concept of gradual abolition through, among other things, banning the international slave trade and making children born into slavery free after a certain date. He also advocated for less physical violence toward enslaved people and better living conditions. According to Monticello, "Although Jefferson continued to advocate for abolition, the reality was that slavery was becoming more entrenched. The slave population in Virginia skyrocketed from 292,627 in 1790 to 469,757 in 1830. Jefferson had assumed that the abolition of the slave trade would weaken slavery and hasten its end. Instead, slavery became more widespread and profitable. In an attempt to erode Virginians' support for slavery, he discouraged the cultivation of crops heavily dependent on slave labor—specifically tobacco—and encouraged the introduction of crops that needed little or no slave labor—wheat, sugar maples, short-grained rice, olive trees, and wine grapes. But by the 1800s, Virginia's most valuable commodity and export was neither crops nor land, but slaves."[9]

And at Monticello, enslaved people spent their entire lives toiling in the fields, with the rhythm of their days constantly regulated by the gong of The Great Clock.

4

James Madison, 1809–1817: Walking Stick

Remarkably, James Madison's close friendship with Thomas Jefferson is common knowledge in the 21st century, thanks to the enormous popularity of the Broadway hit musical *Hamilton*. Their friendship was so significant, when asked to recommend an artifact to represent her president, Montpelier's executive vice president and chief curator, Elizabeth Chew, selected a walking stick that was a bequest from Jefferson to Madison.

According to Montpelier's catalog records, Jefferson received the walking stick while serving as president:

> In 1805, Norfolk physician and merchant John Oliveira Fernandes sent this walking stick, made of rhinoceros horn, to President Thomas Jefferson. When it was initially delivered to Monticello, Jefferson's granddaughter Anne Cary Randolph erroneously believed the walking stick was a gift from Napoleon Bonaparte. However, Jefferson soon learned it was from Fernandes, whom he thanked for the gift. Fernandes replied with his hope that Jefferson's "Love of Natural Philosophy would render so rare a production of the Animal Kingdom acceptable to you. While it might be an usefull companion in your retired & rural excursions at Monticello." Jefferson owned the walking stick for twenty years and in his will stated "I give to my friend James Madison, of Montpelier my gold mounted walking staff of animal horn." Four days after Jefferson's July 4, 1826 death, his grandson Thomas Jefferson Randolph wrote to Madison regarding the "cane a legacy left you by my dear grandfather." Dr. Robley Dunglison, a mutual friend of both men, delivered the walking stick to Montpelier later

that month. After receiving the gift, Madison wrote Randolph, "The article bequeathed to me by your grandfather, had been delivered by Dr. Dunglison, and received with all the feelings due to such a token of the place I held in the friendship of one, whom I so much revered & loved when living and whose memory can never cease to be dear to me."[1]

Madison's friendship with Jefferson began while serving in the Virginia House of Delegates in the heady days just before the Revolutionary War. It was Jefferson who gave Madison's political ideas credibility after the colonies declared their independence from Britain.[2]

Several years after Jefferson's death, Madison recalled how they met. "I was a stranger to Mr. Jefferson till the year 1776, when he took his seat in the first Legislature under the Constitution of Virginia then newly formed; being at the time myself a member of that Body and for the first time a member of any public Body. The acquaintance then made with him was very slight, the

This walking stick represents the close friendship between James Madison and Thomas Jefferson.
PHOTO BY PHILLIP BEAURLINE, COURTESY OF MONTPELIER, A NATIONAL TRUST HISTORIC SITE

distance between our ages being considerable, and other distances much more so. During part of the time whilst he was Governour of the State, a service to which he was called not long after, I had a seat in the Council associated with him. Our acquaintance then became intimate; and a friendship was formed, which was for life, and which was never interrupted in the slightest degree for a single moment."[3]

When Jefferson left the country to serve as an ambassador to France, he asked Madison to take charge of the education of his two fatherless nephews. Between 1784 and 1789, they exchanged one hundred letters, mostly discussing politics. During the 1787 Federal Convention, Madison complied with the secrecy order, which prevented him from sharing details of the debate to create the Constitution, but assured Jefferson that "there can be no doubt but that the result will in some way or other have a powerful effect on our destiny."[4] Madison envisioned a government with three equally powerful branches—executive, legislative, and judicial—which would become the basis of the Constitution. His influence would lead to the nickname "Father of the Constitution," which he argued was inaccurate because the document was "the work of many heads and many hands."[5]

When Jefferson was elected president in 1801, he appointed Madison secretary of state, a position that allowed him to shape the agreement to acquire the Louisiana territory from France, doubling the size of the new nation.[6] During this period, Madison made regular visits to Monticello, just as he had before Jefferson's presidency. The two men lived in close proximity to each other, and both spent the summer congressional recess away from Washington, D.C. The Madisons typically visited Monticello in August or September from 1801 to 1808, a tradition that continued when Madison was elected until the interruption of the War of 1812.[7]

Madison valued Jefferson's opinion, particularly when it came to the architectural details of Montpelier:

Madison wrote to request Jefferson's advice on several occasions: asking him to select appropriate locks, hinges, and pulleys in 1798; requesting a method for coating the brick columns on the portico with plaster in 1800; and sending Jefferson a drawing of proposed renovations to Montpelier in 1808. Madison's phrasing indicated the value he placed on Jefferson's opinion. Regarding the selection of hardware, Madison asked for "such locks & Bolts as your better judgment may chuse." He changed his mind about ordering dovetail rising hinges because "your objection to that sort is so decisive that I can not hesitate to change it for the 5 inch Butt hinge, shewing an iron joint." Madison proposed brass pulleys, "but relying more on your knowledge than my own or my workman's, I must beg you to substitute a better if there be one."[8]

In their briefing paper titled "The Madison-Jefferson Relationship," Hilarie M. Hicks and Elizabeth Ladner further described the nature of the friendship between the two men:

> During Madison's and Jefferson's political lives, opponents were quick to mock, cast aspersions, and condemn Madison for his connections to Jefferson. Newspaper commentary leading up to the election of 1808 included characterizations such as "he is the mere organ or mouthpiece of Mr. Jefferson" and "[w]e knew indeed that he was a man of feeble mind; and had seen with concern that he gave himself up to Mr. Jefferson, without reserving the use of his own judgment."[9]
>
> While Madison has often been depicted as simply Jefferson's lieutenant, recent scholarship (particularly Burstein and Isenberg's *Madison and Jefferson*) has emphasized Madison as a canny politician who orchestrated Jefferson's career, repeatedly persuading him to return to public service when he would have preferred to retreat to Monticello. Even in their later years, Madison continued to be his friend's "pillar of support," as Jefferson described him. Madison served on the Board of Visitors for Jefferson's University of Virginia, and succeeded Jefferson as rector of the University after his death in 1826.[10]

This walking stick, symbolic of 50 years of friendship, was treasured by Madison. According to Montpelier, Madison bequeathed it to Jefferson's grandson, Thomas Jefferson Randolph, who received it upon Madison's death in June 1836.[11] It was passed down through the several generations of the Jefferson family and was donated to Montpelier in 2011.

5

James Monroe, 1817–1825: Desk

A single statement, buried in a Congressional address that was written on this desk, would become a "longstanding tenet" of American foreign policy for decades. "According to family tradition, James Monroe used this mahogany Louis XVI-style desk to write his annual message to Congress in 1823 that included the foreign policy statement later termed the Monroe Doctrine," says Jarod Kearney, assistant director and curator of the James Monroe Museum and Memorial Library. "Monroe bought the desk and associated furniture pieces while serving as Minister to France in the 1790s."[1]

In the address, Monroe "warns European nations that the United States would not tolerate further colonization or puppet monarchs. The doctrine was conceived to meet major concerns of the moment, but it soon became a watchword of U.S. policy in the Western Hemisphere."[2] European powers did not pay attention to the statement at the time, but by the 1850s it would become well known officially as "The Monroe Doctrine." Monroe viewed the United States as a model for the new Latin American republics to emulate, which would be done without the intervention of the Old World:

> The three main concepts of the doctrine—separate spheres of influence for the Americas and Europe, non-colonization, and non-intervention—were designed to signify a clear break between the New World and the autocratic realm of Europe. Monroe's administration forewarned the imperial European powers against interfering in the affairs of the newly independent Latin American states or potential United States territories.[3]

According to family tradition, James Monroe wrote his annual address to Congress at this desk in 1823. That speech included a statement that would become known as "The Monroe Doctrine."

JAMES MONROE MUSEUM

The Monroe Doctrine would be invoked several times in the 19th and 20th centuries, sometimes as a rationalization for imperialist actions. In 1865 the United States used it to justify military and diplomatic pressure in support of Mexican President Benito Juárez, who led a successful revolt against Emperor Maximillian, a figurehead installed by the French government. In 1904, Teddy Roosevelt referenced it when European creditors threatened Latin American countries to collect debt, which led to US Marines being sent to Santo Domingo in 1904, Nicaragua in 1911, and Haiti in 1915.[4]

During the Cuban Missile Crisis in 1962, John F. Kennedy invoked the Monroe Doctrine "symbolically" when the Soviet Union started building missile-launching sites in Cuba. "With the support of the Organization of American States, President John F. Kennedy threw a naval and air quarantine around the island. After several tense days, the Soviet Union agreed to withdraw the missiles and dismantle the sites. Subsequently, the United States dismantled several of its obsolete air and missile bases in Turkey."[5]

The Monroe Doctrine was a young nation's first statement about foreign policy, and the first time the future of the Western Hemisphere was discussed. Although the United States was not able to back up this powerful statement in 1823, a stronger nation would be able to uphold it in the future. It remains Monroe's enduring legacy.[6]

But the connection to one of the nation's most significant foreign policies is not the only fascinating fact about Monroe's desk. In the 20th century a secret compartment was discovered containing letters between Monroe and prominent figures in the American Revolution, including Thomas Jefferson and James Madison. These letters are now part of the Ingrid Westesson Hoes Archive collection at the James Monroe Museum.[7]

6

John Quincy Adams, 1825–1829: Personal Library

Historians often describe John Quincy Adams as "the best prepared president in US history."[1] In addition to spending much of his childhood being groomed for a career in government, he was also an intellectual who accumulated a collection of more than six thousand books during his lifetime. "John Quincy Adams' dedication to knowledge and appetite for books inspired him to collect an impressive library, which is available for study and admiration today," says Kelly Cobble, curator of Adams National Historical Park. "He read the Bible in several languages, and he owned a set of 75 volumes of British Poets, including Cicero, Goethe, Shakespeare, and Chaucer. His collection also includes books on astronomy, gardening, natural history, plants, birds and fish, maritime and constitutional Law, encyclopedias, and dictionaries in many different languages. The breadth [of his collection] is truly astonishing."[2] After his death in 1848, he bequeathed his vast collection of books and personal papers to his son, Charles Francis Adams, who would establish The Stone Library, which is part of the Adams National Historical Park today.

According to Cobble, "John Quincy learned early on the importance of a good library. His mother also knew the power of knowledge and encouraged him in meticulous reading habits and studies. As a young child he was exposed to his father's library." On September 24, 1829, John Quincy wrote in his diary, "At ten years of age, I read Shakespeare's *Tempest*, *As You Like It*, *Merry Wives of Windsor*, *Much Ado about Nothing*, and *King Lear*."[3] During his formative years, John Quincy also watched firsthand as his father and fellow

John Quincy Adams assembled a collection of more than six thousand books during his lifetime.

ADAMS NATIONAL HISTORICAL PARK

patriots rebelled against England and created a new country. He witnessed the Battle of Bunker Hill with his mother, and he "regularly saw soldiers passing through his hometown. The Revolutionary War was not some distant, theoretical event but an immediate and frightening reality."[4]

In spite of being the most qualified presidential candidate, John Quincy is remembered as a relatively unsuccessful one-term president who was "aloof, stubborn, and ferociously independent."[5] He understood the inner workings of government, yet his reluctance to participate in party politics ultimately cost him reelection. Before and after his presidency, however, Adams used his skills as an attorney and diplomat to wield considerable influence in both domestic and foreign policy.

"He used books as tools all his life," Cobble said. "He studied cases from history to prove his present-day cases. He learned seven languages by translating his favorite pieces of literature and collected his favorite works in multiple languages. Books were collected for pleasure, research, and educational value.

For a man who dedicated his life to public service, he acquired books for comfort, inspiration, intellectual gratification, and companionship."[6] For example, when he was appointed to serve as the US Minister to the Netherlands, John Quincy's diary documented that he "looked to the family archive for a 'course of reading' that would orient him to the job, digging through 'large folio volumes containing dispatches from my father during his negotiations in Europe.' To tackle a thorny diplomatic field like Napoleon's Europe, Adams made himself a syllabus and stuck to it—an instinct, that, like rereading the family papers for advice, became a lifelong habit."[7]

After serving as president, John Quincy was persuaded to run for the House of Representatives in 1830. He won the election and enjoyed a much more successful career representing Massachusetts than he had in the White House. He was among the most ardent abolitionists, arguing against the "gag rule" that prevented petitions to end slavery from being heard in Congress. It was rescinded in 1844. He also successfully argued before the Supreme Court on behalf of the men who had mutinied aboard the slave ship Amistad. During this time, his books on maritime and constitutional law would have proven quite valuable.

In 1848 John Quincy had a severe stroke on the House floor. He died two days later and was interred with his parents in the First Congregational Church in his hometown of Quincy, Massachusetts. Always conscious of their lasting legacy, his family would eventually donate his books, papers, and property for a public museum. In its foundation document, the Adams National Historical Park recognizes the significance of the family through the interpretive theme Public Lives, Private Lives: "Generations of Adamses maintained a family ethos of public service, patriotism, education, intellectual achievement, and privileged lineage, which shaped their careers, ideas, achievements, and private lives.[8] John Quincy's personal library is the tangible evidence of these principles.

Andrew Jackson, 1829–1837: Decapitated Figurehead

Widely hailed as the most influential president between George Washington and Abraham Lincoln, Andrew Jackson inspired fond devotion and fierce indignation in equal measure. The latter is best illustrated by the so-called Affair of the Figurehead in 1834.

When the USS *Constitution* entered dry dock at Charlestown Navy Yard on June 24, 1833, Jackson was still enjoying a relatively high approval rating after easily winning reelection against Henry Clay in 1832. The ceremony was delayed so Jackson could attend, but when he arrived in Boston, he became ill and sent Vice President Martin Van Buren to represent him instead.

The ship had become a source of national pride during the War of 1812: "A few weeks after the war broke out in June, while en route to New York, she narrowly escaped a British squadron in a demonstration of brilliant seamanship by her commander, Capt. Isaac Hull. Later that summer, while returning from a successful raiding cruise into Canadian waters, she defeated the British frigate *Guerriere* in a hard-fought, close-range duel. This victory sent a thrill of exultation through the Nation. According to tradition, during the engagement a seaman, on seeing the enemy's shots rebounding from her sides, dubbed the ship 'Old Ironsides.'"[1] By 1828, the ship was condemned as unseaworthy, and plans were made to dismantle her. Thanks in part to Oliver Wendell Holmes's poem "Old Ironsides," the ship was sent to dry dock for extensive repairs instead. Jackson was invited to the ceremony because he too became a War of 1812 hero when he led US forces to a decisive victory at the Battle of New Orleans.

As work progressed on the ship, Jackson's popularity began to decline when his veto to recharter the Second Bank of the United States led to "financial hardship for merchants." When Jesse Duncan Elliott, the commandant of the Charlestown Navy Yard, announced that he had hired local carver Laban S. Beecher to create a figurehead more than 10 feet tall of President Jackson for the USS *Constitution*, there was an immediate backlash.[2] One anonymous letter to the editor of the *Vermont Republican and American Journal* on April 3, 1834, illustrates these strong feelings:

> O fie! forshame! Shall the decendants [*sic*] of those patriots, that spilt their blood, and kindled the flame of the war of Revolution, that brought us out from under the yoke of England's haughty king, disgraces themselves at this rate, to idolize a poor, ignorant old man, that has no trait of character, but to oppress, and destroy the nation! I am an old Revolutionary soldier, and I feel disgraced by this nefarious act—and it will appear a disgraceful act in the eyes of all the nations of the earth. Were I a sailor, I would, sooner than sail in that ship, with that head on, [be] plunged into the crater of Mt. Vesuvius.[3]

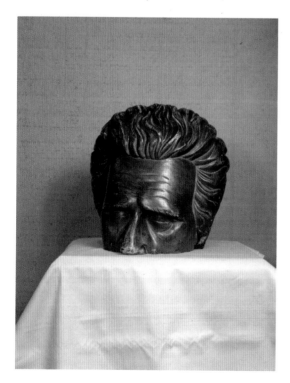

Under cover of darkness, Samuel Worthington Dewey cut the offending figurehead of Andrew Jackson from the bow of the USS *Constitution*.
MUSEUM OF THE CITY OF NEW YORK

Handbills circulated with the phrase, "For God's sake save the ship from this foul disgrace."[4] Although Beecher himself even received threats, the figurehead was completed and installed as planned, and the USS *Constitution* was floated out of dry dock.

Public reception was mostly unkind. The following description appeared in the May 24, 1834 edition of the *Western Carolinian*: "The snarling, ill-natured, insolent, overbearing disposition of the 'great original' is fully expressed in this wooden statue. The artist seems to belong to that school which holds that beauty is ever to be sacrificed to truth."[5]

Then one night, Samuel Worthington Dewey decided to take the matter into his own hands. In the midst of an unusually violent thunderstorm, the 28-year-old "unmoored his boat from Billy Gray's Wharf in Boston, and, with his oar muffled in an old woollen comforter, sculled out into the darkness." He used the man-ropes on the side of the ship to climb aboard. Then he "extended himself on his back, and in this position sawed off the head. While here he saw the sentry on the wharf from time to time looking earnestly toward the spot where he was at work, but the lightning and the storm each time drove the guard back to the shelter of his box."[6]

The next morning, officials were shocked to find a headless figurehead on America's favorite ship. The *Fayetteville Weekly Courier* called the situation "mysterious," saying, "The *Constitution* lies at the Navy Yard, between two seventy-fours,[7] and it is understood that a guard, or watch, is continually kept on board. It seems impossible that the deed could have been executed without discovery, notwithstanding that the night was dark and rainy."[8] The same article reported that Elliot was offering a $1,000 reward for information leading to an arrest.

Dewy waited for the fanfare to die down before packing up the severed head and traveling with it to Washington, D.C. It was his intention to personally deliver it to Jackson, but the president was too sick to see visitors. Instead, he met with Vice President Van Buren, who told him to take it to Mahlon Dickerson, secretary of the Navy. Dickerson was dismayed to discover that there was no actual law against the "beheading of figureheads," so he let Dewey go.[9] Everyone presumed Dickerson discarded the severed head, but he actually took it home. It was handed down for several generations before a curator for the Museum of the City of New York located it outside of Paris in 1998.

The head itself was cut off just below the nose, not at the neck, because there was a thick metal rod in the way. Dodge & Sons of New York created a second head for the figurehead, and it was presumed that the bottom part of the original head was lost.

Fast forward to 2010. The PBS television series *History Detectives* approached the Museum of the City of New York with what they claimed was the bottom part of Jackson's head. *New York Times* journalist Sam Roberts reported, "About 35 years ago, an itinerant collector visited Roy's Marina in Saranac Lake in upstate New York and in exchange for a duck decoy made by the marina's owner, Roy Japp, offered a Sunbeam electric-iron box containing a wooden mouth and chin wrapped in sheepskin. Some papers accompanying the carving identified it as belonging to an Andrew Jackson figurehead on the *Constitution*."[10]

Today, the reunited head along with the original figurehead and its replacement head all reside in the permanent collection of the Museum of the City of New York.

Martin Van Buren, 1837–1841: Desk

Although Martin Van Buren did run for reelection in 1840, he said the two happiest days of his life were the day he took office and the day he surrendered it. Andrew Jackson personally selected him as his successor in 1836, and he won more votes than all three of his competitors combined. He planned to continue Jacksonian-era policies, expecting a smooth, status quo presidency. However, shortly after taking office, a financial crisis rocked the nation, and the hotly contested issues of slavery, tension with Great Britain, and western expansion intensified. With mounting pressure throughout his presidency, it is understandable that he reveled in his 1836 victory, yet felt a sense of relief after his 1840 defeat.

According to Mike Wasko, a museum specialist at the Martin Van Buren National Historic Site, Van Buren was not a strong speaker, so the written word took precedence as he tried to solve the nation's problems. Much of his correspondence would have happened while seated at this mahogany desk. The upper section is a bookcase with a decorated cornice above a rectangular door with three shelves behind it. It is on display at Lindenwald, the Kinderhook, New York, home from which he ran both of his presidential campaigns.

Van Buren is often considered an obscure historical footnote today, but he was a central figure in the political issues of his day. He was instrumental in creating a coalition of Jeffersonian Republicans that would become the new Democratic Party that pushed Jackson to victory in 1828. In recognition of his efforts, Jackson appointed Van Buren as secretary of state and later minister to Britain. Jackson also chose him as a running mate for his second term in 1828.

Martin Van Buren was not a strong speaker, so he relied on the written word to convey his ideas. He used this desk as president, including two "front porch" campaigns that were run out of his home in Kinderhook, New York.

MARTIN VAN BUREN NATIONAL HISTORIC SITE

As the heir apparent, Van Buren actually received eighty-five thousand more votes than Jackson had in the election of 1832.[1]

Jackson may have helped Van Buren get elected, but he was also the main reason he struggled throughout his presidency. Jacksonian policies laid the groundwork for the Panic of 1837, which started prior to Van Buren's inauguration but took a severe turn a few months afterward. Van Buren was forced to make the nation's worst economic crisis to date his top priority. Leading up to the Panic, British banks had stopped investing in the American economy, which ended nearly 20 years of economic growth. Without the British funding, overextended banks began calling in loans. Jackson's 1836 Specie Circular, requiring all federal land sales to be paid with precious metals only and not paper money, made a bad situation worse. In 1837 unemployment reached 25 percent in some areas, and 343 of the 850 banks in the country closed permanently.[2]

The possible annexation of Texas, which would be admitted as a large slaveholding state, also created tension during Van Buren's presidency. In an effort to keep the newly formed Democratic Party from splitting into factions, he broke from Jackson and announced in August 1837 that he was not in favor of annexing Texas. He did, however, continue to support Jackson's Indian Removal Act of 1830, which forcibly removed Native Americans from their ancestral homelands to reservations in the western territories.

By the election of 1840, Van Buren was facing an uphill battle to reelection, and the divisive issues of his first term were not his only obstacle. As the increasingly powerful Whig Party rallied around war hero William Henry Harrison, Van Buren did not stand a chance. He came close to beating Harrison in the popular vote, but he didn't even carry his home state of New York in the electoral vote.

After losing the election, Van Buren returned to Lindenwald to regroup and immediately began planning his triumphant return to the White House in 1844. One can imagine him sitting at this desk, carefully crafting his next presidential campaign. It did not turn out how he had hoped. With Jackson's endorsement and popular support for annexing Texas, James K. Polk easily won the Democratic Party's nomination. Still, he did not give up the idea of being reelected:

> Four years later, the question of new states and slavery had become even more divisive. Van Buren headed a splinter group—the Free-Soil Party—comprised of dissatisfied Democrats, Whigs who opposed their party's nominee, General

Zachary Taylor, and members of the anti-slavery Liberty Party. The Free Soil Party's main issue was opposition to the extension of slavery to the new Western territories. Van Buren had little hope of victory. Taylor won the election convincingly, although the Free Soilers ran well in a number of northern states, including New York, Massachusetts, Ohio, and Illinois.[3]

After this final defeat, Van Buren returned to Lindenwald to become a gentleman farmer for the next 21 years. He spent "the last and happiest days" of his life experimenting with new varieties of vegetables on his 191-acre farm. In 1849, he and his son hired architect Richard Upjohn to renovate and add modern amenities to the home, including running water, a bathroom, and a furnace, which was "one of the first central heating systems in the Hudson Valley."[4] He passed away at Lindenwald in 1862, in the midst of a bitter Civil War, which was fought to resolve many of the issues that plagued Van Buren's presidency.

William Henry Harrison, 1841: Flag Remnant

William Henry Harrison has the dubious honor of having the shortest presidency in American history at just 32 days. But to his contemporaries, he was well known as a war hero who had succeeded in crushing Native American tribes in central Indiana at the Battle of Tippecanoe in 1811. His party capitalized on his military record with the catchy 1840 campaign slogan "Tippecanoe and Tyler too," and he easily won the election as an anti-Jacksonian candidate. Since Harrison had little time to establish a presidential legacy, the best historic treasure to represent him is this flag remnant from the Battle of Tippecanoe that belonged to Captain Spier Spencer.

Harrison's military career began as a young man. His father, Declaration of Independence signer and governor of Virginia, Benjamin Harrison, wanted him to become a doctor. After Benjamin's death in 1791, 18-year-old Harrison left his medical studies and fulfilled his lifelong dream of serving in the military. In 1800 President John Adams appointed him governor of the Indiana Territory, a position in which he excelled. "During the next twelve years he showed great skill in implementing President Adams's chief reason for giving him the job: legally securing as much land as possible from Native Americans. Harrison exploited the tribal chiefs . . . to push through seven treaties in which they ceded their lands."[1] Although historians today are critical of Native American removal policies, Harrison's actions earned him praise from contemporaries who were concerned for the safety of the settlers as they pushed ever westward. Drastically underpaying Native Americans for their land was considered perfectly "legal."

In 1810 Tecumseh, the most powerful chief in the region, confronted Harrison in person about the encroachments on tribal land. "He plainly told the governor that any further incursions into Indian lands would mean war. Harrison insisted that the land had been acquired legally, and Tecumseh began shouting that the governor was a liar."[2] After this encounter, raids on white settlements increased, and Harrison convinced President Madison to let him command the retaliation campaign. On November 6, 1811, 950 men under Harrison's command moved into a position near a small river known as Tippecanoe. Campfires gave away their position before dawn, giving the outnumbered Native Americans the element of surprise. In the midst of the chaos, Harrison mounted his horse and rallied his troops. By midmorning, the counterattack was successful, and the Indians were driven back into the woods.[3]

Captain Spier Spencer, who died during the battle, led a company of mounted riflemen. According to Roger Hardig, vice president of education at the Benjamin Harrison Historic Site, Harrison had appointed Spencer to be the first sheriff of Harrison County, Indiana. "When tensions grew high between the settlers and the Native Americans, Spencer organized the Harrison County Militia known as the 'Yellow Jackets' because of the color of their uniforms, for a campaign against them. Some of the officers brought along younger brothers or sons as part of their commands. Spencer brought his fourteen year old son to serve as orderly and drummer for the 'Yellow Jackets.' The Battle of Tippecanoe . . . ended with Captain Spencer being seriously wounded during the battle. He was shot in the head and when he was being carried off the field he was killed by a second shot."[4] Harrison brought Spencer's son to his own tent and safely transported him to his mother after the war. Spencer's horse and sword, along with this piece of flag, were brought back from the battle and returned to his widow. The flag was passed down through Spencer's youngest daughter's family and eventually donated to the Benjamin Harrison Historic Site.

Harrison commended Spencer for his bravery, and soon the whole country was talking about the battle. "Public reaction to Harrison's actions ran mixed, but was on the whole favorable. There were mutterings of poor generalship and the steep loss of life, but others welcomed the revenge on the Indians whose raids had increased in frequency and severity on the western frontier."[5]

Harrison spent the next 25 years trying to build a career in politics. After losing several elections, he finally became a US Senator in 1824. He was appointed ambassador to Colombia in 1828, but he performed poorly and only

William Henry Harrison's presidency was the shortest in history. He was best known for his role at the Battle of Tippecanoe, which is where this flag remnant came from.
BENJAMIN HARRISON PRESIDENTIAL SITE

lasted a year in that post. After years of living beyond his means, he found himself back in Ohio with mounting debt, a menial job, and few political prospects.

But soon his war experience would earn him a presidential nomination.

The Whig Party watched Andrew Jackson rise to power as a war hero, and they knew it would take another war hero to match his hand-picked successor, Martin Van Buren. They reimagined him as a humble candidate that was relatable:

> They flooded the electorate with posters and badges extolling the virtues of their colorful, down-home "log cabin and hard cider" candidate, the hero of Tippecanoe. In their image remaking of Harrison, the Whigs misrepresented him to the electorate. Harrison was actually from an established Virginia family, a learned student of classics, and a man who enjoyed luxurious living to the point that he was continually in debt. But voters wanted to identify with a war hero who shared their down-to-earth values.[6]

In the end, their tactic worked, and Harrison won four times as many votes as the incumbent.

Although Harrison's death has long been attributed to pneumonia developed after speaking for two hours at his inauguration in cold, wet weather, recent scholarship suggests a different cause: enteric fever. The White House water supply was located downstream from a field where human excrement was deposited daily, creating a breeding ground for deadly bacteria. Harrison had a history of gastrointestinal problems, and treatments of toxic medications and frequent enemas likely exacerbated his condition.[7] Just one month after becoming president, Old Tippecanoe was dead.

10

John Tyler, 1841–1845: Piano

When William Henry Harrison died on April 4, 1841, John Tyler became the first vice president to assume the presidency through the death of a sitting president. In honor of his swearing in, Tyler's wife, Letitia, presented him with this piano, which is part of the collection of Sherwood Forest Plantation, Tyler's family home. A plaque on the piano says: "To My Honored and Adored Husband, On This His Day April 6, 1841—Letitia." This object represents our nation's first test of the concept of a peaceful transition of power.

When the Founding Fathers were crafting a new government, they "spent little time on succession, even though the average human life span was about 35 years. Article II, Section 1 of the Constitution states that if the president is unable to complete his term—either by removal, death, resignation, or inability to discharge the office's duties—the vice president would assume the post."[1] Congress passed the Presidential Succession Act in 1792 which outlined the line of succession beyond the vice president. Next in line was the president pro tempore of the Senate and then the speaker of the House of Representatives.

In 1886 another Presidential Succession Act changed the line of succession to appointed positions, rather than elected positions. Under the new law, after the vice president, the secretary of state was next in line, followed by other departments in the order in which they were created. As positions were renamed and added, the law was amended until Harry S. Truman took office after Franklin Delano Roosevelt's death in 1945. Truman felt that it was more appropriate for elected officials to be first in line. In 1947 a new act set the speaker of the House of Representatives second in line, the president pro tempore of the Senate third, and the secretary of state fourth.

Letitia's choice of a musical instrument to commemorate this significant transition was appropriate for a man who loved music. As a young man, Tyler had aspired to become a concert violinist. Under pressure from his father, he abandoned his dream and became a lawyer instead, but eventually he would find his way back to his first love. "After leaving the presidency, Tyler was able to re-dedicate himself to the violin," said Dr. Jonathan L. Stoltz. "He often entertained guests together with his second wife, a talented guitarist. One author commented that with 15 offspring between his two spouses, he occasionally organized his children into a minstrel band."[2]

This piano symbolizes the first transfer of power due to the death of the president. Vice President John Tyler was sworn in on April 4, 1841, after the death of William Henry Harrison.
PHOTO BY SHELLY LIEBLER

James K. Polk, 1845–1849: Table

James K. Polk's legacy is expansionism. First mentioned in an editorial published in the July–August 1845 issue of *The Democratic Review*, the concept of "manifest destiny" is "the idea that the United States is destined—by God, its advocates believed—to expand its dominion and spread democracy and capitalism across the entire North American continent. The philosophy drove 19th-century US territorial expansion and was used to justify the forced removal of Native Americans and other groups from their homes."[1] But this idea was not just about creating a larger nation by annexing or purchasing territories. The debate about whether these new states would be added to the Union as free states or slaveholding states continued to divide the nation in the years leading to the Civil War.

According to the President James K. Polk Home & Museum, Polk deliberately collected items that reflected his expansionist ideas. He "chose to surround himself with an intentional collection of objects that spoke to the history of conquest: both of the distant past and of the history he was actively writing."[2] This circular slab, presented to him by Dr. Samuel D. Heap, Consul of Tunisia, enveloped both ideas. It was made of marble collected from the ruins of Carthage, but its design was symbolic of Polk's expansion of the United States:

The expansionist President James K. Polk was surely aware of the layers of meaning this unique object carried when he determined to display it prominently in the most public room of his home. On its surface, the design of the marble slab would have resonated with both national and personal significance. The twenty-eighth, twenty-ninth, and thirtieth states (Texas, Iowa, and Wisconsin) had been added to the Union under his Presidency. These three new stars surrounding the eagle were feathers in the eleventh President's cap and surely welcome reminders of his accomplishments as he faced his imminent retirement. . . . Polk wrote to Gwinn Heap, Dr. Heap's son, in gratitude for the unique offering, describing the table as an "admirable" display of skilled workmanship and an object of "peculiar interest." Polk commissioned a table to be built for

Expansionist James K. Polk received this table from Dr. Samuel D. Heap, Consul of Tunisia. It was made from marble collected from the ruins of Carthage, which was destroyed by Roman soldiers in 146 BCE.

PRESIDENT JAMES K. POLK HOME & MUSEUM

the slab, a stylish pedestal centre table with a mahogany veneer. He promised Heap that he would place the piece in his parlour and "carefully preserve it." He did just that.

The raw materials for this remarkable table were in themselves significant statements about Polk, the United States, and the nation's perceived westward destiny. Polk and Dr. Heap understood the marble to have come from the ruins of the ancient city of Carthage, a place Dr. Heap would presumably have experienced as Consul to Tunisia. Across the United States and Europe, the nineteenth century saw a renewed interest in the classical world, and a trend that unfortunately fueled the plundering of ancient sites like Carthage across the Mediterranean and Middle East. Viewed as the seat of western civilization, these ancient cities had long inspired early Americans in shaping the material culture of their new democratic republic. Capturing the tangible history of these ancient sites in Greece, Egypt, and Rome enabled nineteenth-century Americans to materialize a philosophical inheritance of the classical world.[3]

Even before he took office, Polk's presidential campaign focused on his desire to expand the nation's borders. He had "won election with the slogan '54° 40' or fight!' (a reference to the potential northern boundary of Oregon as latitude 54° 40') and called U.S. claims to Oregon 'clear and unquestionable' in his inaugural address."[4] The campaign slogan sounded quite aggressive, but Polk understood that the United States was not interested in going to war with Great Britain over the northern border. In the end, the two countries settled on the 49th parallel, and Polk set his sights on acquiring California from Mexico.

As it turns out, negotiating the Oregon territory deal was much easier than securing California. Polk sent an envoy to Mexico to offer $20,000,000 for the land that would become California, Nevada, Utah, and most of New Mexico, which represented half of Mexico's land. When the envoy was not received, Polk sent General Zachary Taylor to the region, which Mexico interpreted as aggression. Congress declared war, and American forces easily won battle after battle. In 1848 Mexico ceded the land for $5,000,000 less than the original offer.[5]

Polk worked so hard to achieve his presidential goals, it may have cost him his life. Historians have suggested that he might have been physically run down due to overwork. He was also exposed to the same kinds of bacteria in the White House water supply that likely killed William Henry Harrison. Both men had a history of gastrointestinal illness.[6] On his farewell tour, Polk contracted cholera and died just 103 days after leaving office.

Zachary Taylor, 1849–1850: Chair

Zachary Taylor distinguished himself as a military leader, which helped him win the election of 1848, but he struggled to find his way as president. He never had any political ambitions, but his notoriety as a war hero caught the attention of Whig Party leaders, who eventually convinced him to run. When he was elected, he had never even registered to vote.[1]

Taylor's background and uncontroversial stances on many political issues made him an attractive candidate to many different segments of the electorate. "His long military record would appeal to northerners; his ownership of a hundred slaves would lure southern votes. He had not committed himself on troublesome issues. The Whigs nominated him to run against the Democratic candidate, Lewis Cass, who favored letting the residents of territories decide for themselves whether they wanted slavery."[2]

When he was elected, Taylor was the most popular man in the country because his many victories during the Mexican War (1846–1848) were fresh in the minds of most Americans. In spite of being outnumbered most of the time, Taylor's men kept winning battles under his leadership. His reputation as a war hero culminated at the Battle of Buena Vista in 1847. Mexican General Santa Anna assembled 20,000 troops to fight against just 6,000 men under Taylor. When it was all said and done, 1,800 Mexicans were killed, but Taylor lost only 672.

To commemorate this decisive win, the general's men had this chair made for him from wood taken from the battlefield at Buena Vista and later presented it to him.[3] The chair's back, seat, and arms are upholstered with

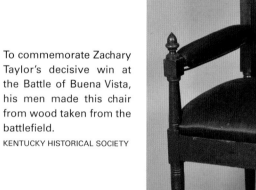

To commemorate Zachary Taylor's decisive win at the Battle of Buena Vista, his men made this chair from wood taken from the battlefield.

KENTUCKY HISTORICAL SOCIETY

horsehair. The arms and back of the chair are adorned with four acorn finials, which come from the oak tree and are symbolic of strength, perseverance, and courage. All parts of the oak tree, including its leaves, are associated with victorious Roman generals and military leadership.[4]

Soon after the victory at Buena Vista, everyone was talking about this remarkable war hero:

> The word of how Old Zack had fought alongside his troops in hand-to-hand combat at both Monterey and Buena Vista spread like a prairie fire across the nation. Taylor was compared to American war heroes George Washington and Andrew Jackson in the popular press. Stories were told about his informal dress, the tattered straw hat on his head, and the casual way he always sat atop his beloved horse, "Old Whitey," while shots buzzed around his head.[5]

Taylor considered himself an independent and a strong nationalist. He disagreed with Andrew Jackson's decision to kill the Second Bank of the United States, and although he was a slave owner, he did not think it was practical to add more slaveholding states to the Union when cotton and sugar could not be grown in western climates. The Whig Party decided to focus his campaign exclusively on his war record:

> Relying on Taylor's national appeal as a war hero, the Whigs presented him as an ideal man "without regard to creeds or principles" and ran him without any platform. This tactic attracted criticism from many directions. Some thought that Taylor had no position while others felt that he lacked political experience and knowledge. Moreover, there were people who believed that his military success was not enough to qualify him for President. Taylor's refusal to actively campaign allowed him to stand above party politics, although his supporters waged a vigorous battle on his behalf.[6]

In spite of these concerns, Taylor won the election with 46 percent of the popular vote in the North and 51 percent in the South.

Slavery in the western territories was the most contested issue of the day, yet Taylor did not mention it at all in his inaugural address. Taylor's policy about new states was to let them decide whether or not they wanted to permit slavery. When California applied for statehood as a free state, the Union was evenly divided with 15 slaveholding states and 15 free states. Adding another free state would disrupt the delicate balance, causing some southern lawmakers to call for a secession convention. As a strong nationalist, Taylor said he would "hang anyone who tried to disrupt the Union by force or by conspiracy."[7]

To avoid conflict, Congress began working on a compromise. Before a solution could be reached, Taylor was dead. Although eating a large quantity of cherries and drinking iced milk has been linked to his death, it is likely that Taylor was yet another victim of the White House's contaminated water supply.[8] After coming down with severe stomach pain that doctors diagnosed as "cholera morbus," or acute gastroenteritis today, he died on July 9, 1850. His successor, Millard Fillmore, would sign the Compromise of 1850 into law.

13

Millard Fillmore, 1850–1853: Engraving of Debate

The biggest political question of the antebellum era was slavery. Millard Fillmore's unexpected presidency was defined by the Compromise of 1850. As vice president, he presided over the debate, and it would become the first bill he signed into law after Zachary Taylor died and he became president.

As Taylor was dying, the pressure mounted for Fillmore. "When the President finally passed away, Fillmore passed a sleepless night, brooding over what lay ahead. The nation was embroiled in a sectional crisis of the first order, and all eyes would be on the new President. At noon the next day, he took the oath of office in the Capitol and left without giving a speech."[1] He knew the biggest challenge he faced was slavery, and he supported compromise to preserve the Union. A few days before Taylor's death, Fillmore said that, if needed, he intended to use his role as vice president to break a tie vote in the Senate in favor of the law.

Rachelle Moyer Francis, board member at the Millard Fillmore Presidential Site and author of *Will the Real Millard Fillmore Please Stand Up?*, suggested that the best representation of Fillmore's presidency is the famous image portraying the debate over the Compromise of 1850. This engraving, titled "The United States Senate, A.D. 1850," was drawn by P. F. Rothermel and engraved by R. Whitechurch. It depicts the debate over the Compromise of 1850 in the Old Senate chamber, with Henry Clay making his arguments and Millard Fillmore presiding over the Senate chamber as vice president. This moment, captured in time by a daguerreotype which Rothermel used as inspiration for his drawing, represents Clay's "last significant act as a senator." Also pictured

This engraving, titled "The United States Senate, A.D. 1850," was drawn by P. F. Rothermel and engraved by R. Whitechurch. It depicts the debate over the Compromise of 1850, with Henry Clay making his arguments and Millard Fillmore presiding over the Senate chamber as vice president.

LIBRARY OF CONGRESS

is Daniel Webster, sitting with his head in his hand on the left, and John C. Calhoun, standing third from the right. Clay, Webster, and Calhoun were known as the "Great Triumvirate," who were desperately trying to reach a compromise to prevent war.[2]

After Zachary Taylor's untimely death, Fillmore became president and signed the Compromise of 1850 into law. "Fillmore knowingly abdicated his future in politics by signing it, hoping to preserve the Union," said Francis. "He despised slavery, but as a lawyer, hoped for a legal way to end it. We also know that Fillmore joined the Adamses as the only three of the first 13 presidents who never owned a slave."[3]

Congress wanted to preserve the Union at all costs, and the Compromise of 1850 was designed to do that. As with many compromises, everyone got something, but no one was truly happy with it. Senators Henry Clay and Stephen Douglas were the primary architects of the deal, which contained five key laws. It settled the issue of slavery in Washington, D.C., by permitting it, but banning the slave trade itself in the nation's capitol. California was admitted as a free state, as they had originally requested. Utah and New Mexico became territories and would be allowed to decide the slavery question themselves. A border was established between the new state of Texas and the New Mexico territory. An aggressive new Fugitive Slave Law passed without much debate, but it would eventually become the most controversial part of the legislation.[4]

The original Fugitive Slave Law from 1793 "authorized local governments to seize and return people who had escaped slavery to their owners while imposing penalties on anyone who had attempted to help them gain their freedom. . . . The Fugitive Slave Act of 1850 compelled all citizens to assist in the capture of runaway slaves and denied enslaved people the right to a jury trial. It also placed control of individual cases in the hands of federal commissioners, who were paid more for returning a suspected slave than for freeing them, leading many to argue the law was biased in favor of Southern slaveholders."[5]

When signing the bills, Fillmore believed it to be a "triumph of interparty cooperation that had kept the Union intact." Public opinion disagreed:

> Many Americans, however, did not see it that way. For those with strong feelings about slavery, the compromise seemed to offer something for everyone to dislike. Northern abolitionists were enraged by the Fugitive Slave Law, and several states subsequently passed laws prohibiting its enforcement. Southern proslavery forces, meanwhile, were dismayed by the restrictions on the practice in California and the District of Columbia. They also doubted the government's commitment to enforce the Fugitive Slave Law. Fillmore struggled to keep these disparate factions appeased.[6]

In an effort to appease the South, Fillmore wanted the Fugitive Slave Law to be strictly enforced. To ease northern fears, he ordered the military to strengthen federal forts in South Carolina. "Unfortunately, by trying to please everyone, Millard Fillmore, it seemed, could please no one. The Whig Party began to fall apart from the strain of all the conflicting points of view on slavery."[7] Frustrated and weary from criticism all around, Fillmore did not actively seek reelection, and the Whigs nominated General Winfield Scott instead. Many historians now view the Compromise of 1850, Fillmore's most significant accomplishment, as prolonging regional divisions rather than actually working toward solving them.

Franklin Pierce, 1853–1857: Kansas-Nebraska Act

Like many presidents in the years leading to the Civil War, Franklin Pierce's administration was consumed with the issue of slavery and keeping the Union intact. Under his leadership, the Kansas-Nebraska Act would become both "one of the most crucial pieces of legislation in American history" and the document that would "set the nation on its path to civil war."[1] Officially titled "An Act to Organize the Territories of Nebraska and Kansas," this is the original document that Pierce signed on May 30, 1854. It is housed as part of the bound congressional records in the National Archives.

That election year, the bitterly divided Democratic Party had trouble settling on a candidate. Pierce won on the 35th ballot at the national convention. He seemed like the perfect choice: "handsome, sociable, a fine speaker, a Mexican-American War veteran—above all a man not forceful enough to ruffle anyone's feathers."[2] The campaign quickly turned personal as both candidates tried to avoid their party's position on slavery. General Winfield Scott's supporters accused Pierce of cowardice during the war and claimed he had a drinking problem. Pierce's supporters revived old stories about Scott's refusal to duel Andrew Jackson and claimed he would lead the country as a military dictator. Pierce easily won what the contemporary media called "the most ludicrous, ridiculous, and uninteresting presidential campaign ever."[3]

The Kansas and Nebraska territories were not yet settled when Pierce took office, but there were many people interested in relocating. The biggest obstacle to settlement was the Missouri Compromise of 1820, which banned slavery in the region. Pro-slavery Southerners wanted the law overturned, so

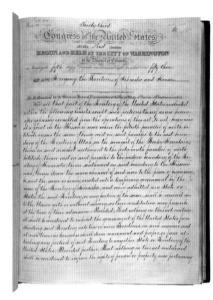 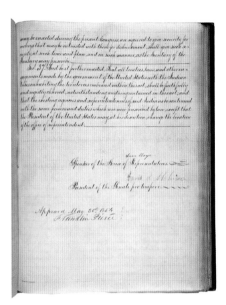

The Kansas-Nebraska Act of 1854 defined Franklin Pierce's presidency and sparked a series of skirmishes that became known as "Bleeding Kansas."
NATIONAL ARCHIVES AND RECORDS ADMINISTRATION

Stephen Douglas introduced legislation in 1854 that would allow the people who lived in a territory to decide for themselves whether or not they would permit slavery.

Pierce believed that most of the compromise legislation would be ruled unconstitutional, so initially he tried to convince Douglas to leave it up to the Supreme Court. Douglas refused, believing that the only way to keep the Southern states from seceding was a legislative repeal. Congressional pressure ultimately swayed him, and, after heated debate, Congress passed and Pierce signed the Kansas-Nebraska Act, lifting the slavery ban north of the latitude 36°30'. The original document, officially titled "An Act to Organize the Territories of Nebraska and Kansas" with Pierce's signature on the second page, is part of the National Archives and Records Administration's collection.

The effect of the new law was far reaching and completely changed the political landscape:

In its wake, one party, the Whigs, was destroyed, while a new and strictly Northern party, the Republicans, came into being, soon to be led by a lawyer named Abraham Lincoln. On the other hand, the Democrats were gravely weakened, especially Douglas and Pierce, as Northern Democrats split over the measure. Intended to lessen controversy, the act did the opposite, increasing national debates and tensions over slavery between North and South.[4]

Kansas became the next showdown for the debate. Since popular sovereignty would now decide the slavery question in the new territories, proslavery and abolitionist activists flooded the region in an attempt to influence the vote. Pierce removed Andrew Reeder, his original choice for territorial governor, and installed pro-slavery Wilson Shannon instead. In response, the abolitionists tried to set up their own government. Escalating tensions soon led to violence, and the period between 1855 and 1859 became known as "Bleeding Kansas." More than 50 people were killed during that period.

What happened in Kansas overshadowed Pierce's entire presidency. Although he wanted to run for reelection, his handling of this situation cost him his political future. Pierce considered his presidency a work in progress, and he desperately wanted a second term to make amends for his earlier shortcomings. His party, however, would have none of it. His poor handling of domestic and foreign affairs did little to secure him support in the Democratic Party. Consequently, his party abandoned him as a presidential candidate in 1856 and chose James Buchanan.[5] Most historians today view him as one of the worst presidents in history, "an inept chief executive whose traditional style of leadership failed in the face of the massive electoral divisions over slavery and the aggressiveness of Southerners."[6] Theodore Roosevelt described him as "a servile tool of men worse than himself . . . ever ready to do any work the slavery leaders set him."[7]

When the Civil War broke out, Pierce supported the North, but not Abraham Lincoln. He publicly blamed Lincoln for the war, which destroyed many of his friendships. His death in 1869 attracted very little attention.[8]

James Buchanan, 1857–1861: Law Books

After tensions continued to escalate during Franklin Pierce's administration, James Buchanan's election inspired hope that he would be the man to successfully steer the country away from a national crisis. Although he had decades of experience as a lawyer and politician, Buchanan was not the man to lead the nation forward. Not only did he fail to ease the tension, but the nation was even more divided at the end of his four years in office, and a landmark Constitutional case would define his presidency.

According to Patrick Clarke, director of President James Buchanan's Wheatland in Lancaster, Pennsylvania, Buchanan was known for being a strict constructionist. These law books, which are part of Wheatland's collection, represent his formative years as an attorney, when he was building the foundation for his political views. "The law was his bible," Clarke said. "Note that one of the US Law books states it covers the laws up to 3 March 1845. These are the books he used during his early years in practice."[1]

Buchanan was born into a life of privilege, which prepared him well for both his political and law careers. "The Buchanans could afford to send James to good schools, and after graduating with honors from Dickinson College, James Buchanan studied law. His legal and political careers moved forward together.[2] In W. U. Hensel's speech "James Buchanan as a Lawyer," given on March 28, 1912, he quotes Buchanan: "I can say, with truth, that I have never known a harder student than I was at that period of my life. I studied law, and nothing but law, or what was essentially connected with it. I took pains to understand thoroughly, as far as I was capable, everything which I read; and in order to fix it upon my memory and give myself the habit of extempore speaking, I almost every evening took a lonely walk, and embodied the ideas which I had acquired during the day in my own language. This gave me a habit of extempore speaking. . . . I derived great improvement from this practice."[3]

His hard work would pay great dividends. "From the very outset of his career at the bar Mr. Buchanan secured a large clientage and what was then a profitable practice," Hensel said, "and he retained both until the larger activities of official life claimed his exclusive attention. Between 1813 and 1829 his professional emoluments ranged from $938 per annum—a fine start for the first year—to $7,915 in 1818."[4] Hensel quotes an unattributed early Lancaster judge in his speech, who describes how Buchanan's qualities combined to make him a fine lawyer:

> There was a combination of physical and intellectual qualities that contributed to make him a powerful advocate. He was more than six feet in height, with a fine, imposing figure, a large, well-formed head, a clear complexion, beautiful skin, large blue eyes, which he turned obliquely upon those he was addressing, looking so honest and earnest as to engage their sympathy by his gaze alone; then his voice was strong, resonant and not unmusical, and his elocution, though very deliberate, flowed on like a full river in a constant current. Add to this, he was a logician and indefatigable in his preparation of his case. In fact, he was cut out by nature for a great lawyer, and I think was spoiled by fortune when she made him a statesman.[5]

Buchanan was first elected to public office in 1820 when he became a congressman for Pennsylvania. He quickly became a "notable constitutional lawyer" and served the House Judiciary Committee.[6] In 1833, he became a senator. Personally, he did not support slavery, but he simultaneously "claimed that the Constitution upheld the right of Southerners to own slaves and saw it as America's duty to protect slavery in the South. Throughout his political career, Buchanan remained largely sympathetic to Southern interests on slavery-related issues."[7]

He wanted to run for president in 1844, 1848, and 1852, but was not successful until 1856. "A smooth, pleasantly dull conservative, he upset few people," writes William Cooper, professor of history at Louisiana State University, for The Miller Center. "Above all, Buchanan was from the North, yet he maintained ideological ties to the South."[8] This proved to be a winning combination.

James Buchanan's law books represent his formative years as an attorney, when he was building the foundation for his political views.
PRESIDENT JAMES BUCHANAN'S WHEATLAND, COURTESY OF LANCASTERHISTORY, LANCASTER, PENNSYLVANIA

In his inaugural address, Buchanan again referenced his strict adherence to the Constitution while clarifying his position on slavery: "It is the imperative and indispensable duty of the government of the United States to secure to every resident inhabitant the free and independent expression of his opinion by his vote. This sacred right of each individual must be preserved. That being accomplished, nothing can be fairer than to leave the people of a territory free from all foreign interference to decide their own destiny for themselves, subject only to the Constitution of the United States."[9] A few days later, the Supreme Court announced the Dred Scott decision, which classified enslaved people as property with no rights under the law. The court also announced that the Missouri Compromise was unconstitutional, a decision Buchanan had influenced. Slavery could no longer be banned in new territories or states, which enraged abolitionists.

When elected, Buchanan had pledged to be a one-term president. His final days in office set the tone for what was to come: a bloody civil war. In an attempt to avoid alienating anyone, he wound up pleasing no one. Although his refusal to take action against the South "averted war for the time being, it also enabled the new Confederate government to begin operations. Buchanan seemed eager to get out of the White House before the real disasters ensued.[10]

After he left office, Buchanan's portrait had to be removed from the Capitol after it was repeatedly damaged by vandals. According to Hensel's 1912 speech, Buchanan had no regrets about how he conducted himself as president. "A year or two before he died, reviewing his career at the bar and in public life, Mr. Buchanan wrote, 'I pursued a settled, consistent line of policy from the beginning to the end, and, on reviewing my past conduct, I do not recollect a single important measure which I should desire to recall, even if this were in my power. Under this conviction, I have enjoyed a tranquil and cheerful mind, notwithstanding the abuse I have received, in full confidence that my countrymen would eventually do justice.'"[11] After his term as president ended, Buchanan retreated to his home at Wheatland, where he died in 1868.

Abraham Lincoln, 1861–1865: Chair from Ford's Theatre

On April 14, 1865, Abraham Lincoln wanted to escape the pressures of being a commander in chief during wartime by going to see a play. General Robert E. Lee had surrendered five days earlier, so perhaps Lincoln felt like taking the night off to celebrate, or at least to redirect his thoughts from the bloody toll of the war. As he was enjoying Tom Taylor's satirical comedy *Our American Cousin* from a private box at Ford's Theatre, John Wilkes Booth crept up behind him and shot him at close range. Today Lincoln's blood still stains the upholstery of the chair he was sitting in that night.

Presidents, especially those who were assassinated, are often viewed as larger-than-life figures. When a president is killed, the outpouring of emotion across party lines tends to deify these men, as the nation as a whole mourns the sudden death of its leader. Their faults are often minimized, while their strengths are accentuated, and the reality of their administrations tend to become a bit skewed. Lincoln is no exception.

The stakes were high in the election of 1860. Lincoln was a relatively moderate candidate who did not want to interfere with slavery in the Southern states, but he also did not want to admit new slaveholding states to the Union. Although he was morally opposed to slavery, he hoped it would eventually become extinct over time on its own. The future of slavery became the central issue in the election. Four major candidates split the votes, and Lincoln won just 40 percent of the popular vote and 59 percent of the electoral votes. The election results clearly defined regional opinions about slavery. In the South, Lincoln barely won any votes, partially because his name did not even appear

Abraham Lincoln was assassinated while sitting in this chair in the President's Box of Ford's Theatre on April 15, 1865.

on the ballot in some districts. John Breckinridge, the pro-slavery candidate who was serving as James Buchanan's vice president, easily carried the South. John Bell, a Constitutional Union candidate, won Tennessee, Kentucky, and Virginia, while Northern Democrat Stephen Douglass carried only Missouri. Although he did not receive the majority of the votes, Lincoln won the election, marking the first time "the nation had elected a president who headed a completely sectional party and who was committed to stopping the expansion of slavery."[1]

Free Northern states had made Lincoln's victory possible, and although the Republicans had not won control of Congress, the Southern states feared the new president would persuade the border states to emancipate their enslaved people. If only free states were permitted to join the Union moving forward, it would not be long before there were enough free states to ratify an amendment banning slavery. On December 20, 1860, South Carolina held a convention that unanimously passed a resolution to secede from the United States. Texas, Louisiana, Mississippi, Alabama, Georgia, and Florida soon followed. It was no coincidence that these states had the highest proportion of white slaveholders.

The seceded states began occupying federal property, including Fort Sumter in Charleston, South Carolina. When Lincoln attempted to have much-needed food supplies sent to the men inside Fort Sumter, the Confederate president, Jefferson Davis, interpreted it as an act of aggression and instructed his forces to open fire if the United States refused to surrender. The Civil War had begun.

Although modern historians view Lincoln as one of the greatest presidents of all time, he was actually rather unpopular. He and his wife, Mary Todd Lincoln, were criticized from all sides both politically and personally. Some of his adversaries thought he was going too far, while others thought that he was not going far enough. It seemed that Lincoln could not win, no matter which path he chose. The Abraham Lincoln Presidential Library & Museum conveys the complexity of Lincoln's struggle with public opinion in its Whispering Gallery:

> To physically illustrate [his unpopularity] and communicate the pressures upon the Lincolns, a dark, crooked, unsettling hallway was constructed through which the visitors pass. Along the walls you will discover actual political cartoons of the period—which was quite an art form then—as well as genuine quotes from newspapers regarding the Lincolns' appearance, manners, and policies. As you

walk through you will hear voices whispering some of the many mean things that were said about the Lincolns in their first year and half in office.[2]

In spite of the opposition he faced, Lincoln made the bold move to issue the Emancipation Proclamation on January 1, 1863, which freed enslaved people in the rebellion states. This marked a turning point in the war, which had been primarily focused on "preserving the Union." The document also paved the way for the creation of the United States Colored Troops, which permitted 179,000 African American men to voluntarily serve in the Army, and almost 37,000 would lose their lives.[3]

As the war raged on, and the death toll began to pile up, Lincoln held fast to his belief that the only way to end the war was reunification without slavery. Although some called for the suspension of the 1864 election because of the war, Lincoln insisted that it go on as an important symbol of free government. Lincoln won reelection easily against Union general George McClellan with 55 percent of the popular vote and 212 electoral votes.

By the spring of 1865, the Union was well on its way to victory over the Confederacy, and Lincoln had successfully led a campaign for Congress to pass the Thirteenth Amendment, which abolished slavery. As he prepared for his second inaugural address on March 4, many were calling for vengeance against the South and eagerly anticipated what he would say on the matter. Approximately thirty thousand people assembled to hear his speech, which ended with an earnest appeal for healing and a call to see the war to its conclusion: "With malice toward none with charity for all . . . let us strive on to finish the work we are in to bind up the nation's wounds . . . to do all which may achieve and cherish a just, and a lasting peace, among ourselves, and with all nations."[4]

Less than a month later, Lincoln was sitting in Ford's Theatre, enjoying a play. The permanent exhibition at the Abraham Lincoln Presidential Library and Museum vividly re-creates the scene in the moments just before the assassination:

> Mary and Abraham Lincoln are seated, holding hands, and watching the action on the stage below. Lincoln appears much older and frailer, but there is a hint of a smile on his face. . . . John Wilkes Booth is just entering the presidential box. His hand is suspiciously reaching under his jacket. Mary holds his hand, and at a few minutes before ten hugged him and asked, "What will Miss Harris think of my hanging on to you so?" Lincoln turned to her with a tender reply, "She won't think anything about it." Those were the last words Mary would hear from

her husband. Moments later, at approximately 10:15 p.m., John Wilkes Booth gained entrance to the presidential box, and placing a derringer pistol behind the president's left ear, shot him at point-blank range. Lincoln slumped forward, mortally wounded, while Booth leapt to the stage and made his escape. Mary's screams echoed through the stunned theatre.

After the assassination, the theater and all its contents were seized by the federal government. For two years, the bloody chair was kept in the private office of Secretary of War Edwin Stanton. It was transferred to the Smithsonian in 1867, where it remained in storage for more than 50 years. In 1927, Blanche Chapman Ford, widow of theater manager Harry Clay Ford, petitioned for the return of the chair. The War Department ordered the Smithsonian to give it back to Mrs. Ford, who sold it at auction in 1929. Henry Ford purchased it for his museum for $2,400. He also purchased the entire Logan County, Illinois, courthouse, where Lincoln had practiced law, and moved it to Greenfield Village, the outdoor living-history component of his new museum. The chair was displayed in the courthouse until 1979, when it moved into the Museum.

By the 1990s, the fabric on the chair was badly deteriorating. As conservators prepared for its conservation treatment, fabric samples were analyzed to determine both the composition of the fabric and to confirm the cause of the extensive stains. According to the Henry Ford Museum, "A preliminary test for blood using the reagent Benzidine yielded positive results in two areas—the front of the seat and near the upper portion of the back. More extensive testing would be required to provide additional information regarding its origin. Given the chair's well-documented history and a lack of available samples of the President's blood and DNA, The Henry Ford has decided not to pursue further testing."[5]

In 2006, the chair joined such iconic artifacts as George Washington's camp bed and the Rosa Parks bus in an exhibition called "With Liberty and Justice for All." Today, it still provides a visceral connection to the past for visitors. The Museum's website explains its power: "For decades, visitors have sought out the Lincoln rocker at The Henry Ford. They are drawn to it not simply because of its role at the center of a tragedy, but as a symbol of a beloved president. The chair provides a unique sense of awe and reverence—it's a lasting personification of the sacrifice Abraham Lincoln made in fashioning a more perfect Union."[6]

17

Andrew Johnson, 1865–1869: Impeachment Note

A ndrew Johnson was never supposed to become president.
Lincoln chose him as a running mate because he was afraid he would lose his reelection campaign in 1864 if he didn't find a way to gain more support. As the only Southern senator who had sided with the Union, Johnson became an instant villain in the South and a hero in the North. Lincoln understood that picking Johnson as his vice president could potentially merge War Democrats and Republicans into a "Union" party, which would ultimately lead to victory.[1] Just a few weeks into his second term, Lincoln was assassinated, and Johnson suddenly became president. The plot had included plans to kill Johnson as well, but would-be assassin George Andrew Atzerodt lost his nerve after a night of drinking.[2] Instead of languishing in the office of the vice president, or being murdered, Johnson became president during a pivotal time in our nation's history for which he was woefully unprepared. His inability to navigate the postwar political landscape led to the dubious honor of being the first president to be impeached.

Congress was not in session for the first eight months of Johnson's presidency, which allowed him to push through his own policies, ranging from routine pardons to allowing "black codes" to be set up in the Southern states. Although the reunited Southern states were required to adhere to the abolition of slavery, as defined in the Thirteenth Amendment, "black codes" allowed white people to create a system that continued to oppress former enslaved people. For example, South Carolina forced black people to pay an annual tax between $10 and $100 to hold any occupation other than a farmer or servant.[3]

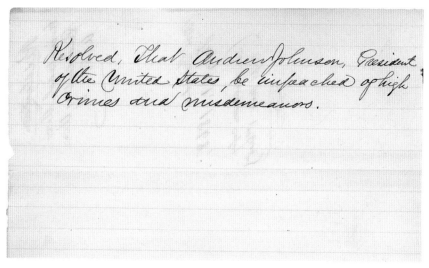

Andrew Johnson became the first president to be impeached on February 21, 1868.
NATIONAL ARCHIVES AND RECORDS ADMINISTRATION

When Congress came back into session, it began to take steps to stop Johnson:

> In 1866, Congress passed the Freedmen's Bureau Bill, providing shelter and provisions for former slaves and protection of their rights in court, as well as the Civil Rights Act, defining all persons born in the United States as citizens. Congress also passed the Fourteenth Amendment to the Constitution, authorizing the federal government to protect the rights of all citizens. Each of these—except the amendment—Congress passed over President Johnson's veto. In a final humiliating gesture, Congress passed the Tenure of Office Act, which stripped the President of the power to remove federal officials without the Senate's approval. In 1867, Congress established a military Reconstruction program to enforce political and social rights for Southern blacks.[4]

The Tenure of Office Act in particular infuriated Johnson. He embarked on a nationwide tour to try to build support by campaigning for congressional candidates who would vote in favor of his own political agenda. When his efforts failed, he decided to challenge the act directly by firing Secretary of War Edwin Stanton. According to the National Archives, "On February 21, 1868, this resolution to impeach President Andrew Johnson was written on a scrap of paper and introduced in the U.S. House of Representatives. Three days later the House voted 128–47 to adopt the resolution."[5] He was charged with 11 articles of impeachment, most for high crimes and misdemeanors related to violating the Tenure of Office Act, including intent to violate the act; conspiracy with Stanton's replacement, Lorenzo Thomas; making speeches "with a loud voice, certain intemperate, inflammatory, and scandalous harangues" with the intent to disgrace Congress; and declaring the 39th Congress unconstitutional because it did not represent all of the states.[6]

During his impeachment trial, Johnson's attorneys argued that he had fired Stanton to test the constitutionality of the Tenure of Office Act, and "his action constituted neither a high crime nor a misdemeanor by any sensible definition of the terms."[7] It was unclear whether Johnson's actions constituted impeachable offenses, which ultimately worked in his favor. A deeply divided Senate voted not to convict him. But the damage had been done. Johnson served the rest of his term wielding relatively little power, ushering in an era of Congressional strength and a weakened presidency for many administrations to come.

Ulysses S. Grant, 1869–1877: Inkwell

Ulysses S. Grant was elected president without having any political experience, and he rejected party politics, making it quite ironic that an elephant-shaped inkwell that he owned was possibly the inspiration for the symbol of the Republican Party. He was a Civil War hero who disagreed with Andrew Johnson's handling of Reconstruction immediately following the war. He aligned himself with policies supported by the Radical Republicans, who favored African American civil rights and barring Confederate leaders from holding office. "He possessed a coherent political philosophy mirrored in Lincoln's Republican Party that won the war, freed the enslaved people, and saved the Republic."[1] But Grant refused to blindly put political party first. Toward the end of his second term, he signed the unpopular Civil Rights Act, a law that prohibited racial segregation on public transportation and accommodations. Many thought his support was damaging to the Republican Party, but "Grant saw the act as a stand taken on principle," said Melissa Trombley-Prosch, historian of the Friends of the Ulysses S. Grant Cottage.[2] Politics, it seemed, were irrelevant.

The inkwell remained in the Grant family until it was sold at auction by Sotheby's in 2001. According to the catalog, it was used by Grant in the White House, "where he frequently entertained the cartoonist Thomas Nast, who had been devoted to Grant since the Civil War. When Grant was elected to the presidency in 1868, he credited his victory to two factors: 'The sword of Sheridan and the pencil of Thomas Nast.'" The elephant as a symbol of the Republican Party first appeared in a Nast cartoon in the *Harper's Weekly* issue of November 7, 1874, just before the midterm elections of Grant's second term. "Partly inspired by a false story that reported a mass escape of animals from New York's Central Park Zoo, Nast's cartoon illustrated the fable 'An ass having put on a lion's skin roamed about in the forest and amused himself by frightening all the foolish animals he met within his wanderings.' One of the frightened animals was an elephant, which was labeled 'The Republican Vote.' Nast used the same symbol in a second cartoon later that same month, and the device spread thereafter into widespread acceptance."[3]

Nast's personification of the political parties as animals was ingenious. "It was Nast's insight to present American politics as one big, messy menagerie," said Jackson Arn, writing for CNN. "Like the best satirists, he ridiculed his own side almost as gleefully as he did his opponents'—and so, he reimagined the GOP as a weak, panicky creature that was constantly lumbering off in the wrong direction, its size more of a liability than an asset."[4]

Nast is also credited with the creation of the donkey as the symbol of the Democratic Party, which he mocked the same as the elephant. "Nast's donkeys fare no better; a typical cartoon from 1879 shows the stubborn beast dangling by the tail, about to fall into an abyss of 'financial chaos.' More often than not, in fact, his cartoons depict elephants and donkeys only a hair's breadth away from chaos—a pretty fair assessment of Republican and Democratic leadership during the Gilded Age."[5]

Sotheby's described President Grant's inkwell as a "black-painted standing elephant with gilt-metal blanket lifting to reveal a brass and glass inkpot."
PHOTOGRAPH COURTESY OF SOTHEBY'S, INC. ©

Rutherford B. Hayes, 1877–1881: Morgan Silver Dollar

Following the Civil War, the national debt had increased over 4,000 percent, and much of the war had been financed by printing "greenbacks," paper money that was backed by the federal government, rather than actual gold or silver. "Reflecting the perceived willingness or capacity of the federal government, at some future date, to redeem greenbacks in gold, their value dropped below par and fluctuated, bringing gold out of circulation and the United States off the gold standard."[1]

The Panic of 1873, which occurred between Hayes's second and third terms as Ohio governor, created an economic depression that lasted for the next four years. The panic began after a stock market crash in Europe led to investors selling their interests in American projects, especially the railroad industry which had been considerably financed by borrowed money. New York City bank Jay Cooke and Company, which had invested a great deal of money in the railroad industry, went bankrupt. As customers across the country flocked to their own banks to demand their cash, a total of one hundred banks failed nationwide.[2]

Two competing economic theories emerged to help ease the financial crisis:

Advocates of inflation (usually midwestern and southern farmers and businessmen who were in debt) wished to increase the number of greenbacks in circulation while creditors (often northeasterners whose banks provided them with an adequate money supply and who would profit from deflation) wished to return to the stability of the gold standard and redeem greenbacks at face value. The hard money (gold) advocates tended to see this conflict in moral rather than in economic terms, as a struggle between honest and dishonest money. Those who favored soft money spoke in terms of justice for the so-called producing classes.[3]

Although Hayes was an investor in real estate and therefore a debtor, he supported the 1875 Specie Resumption Act, which "provided for the redemption of paper currency in gold or silver and a reduction in the amount of outstanding paper bills, the so-called 'Greenbacks,' beginning in 1879. Restoring convertibility was a necessary step in the re-establishment of the gold standard."[4] Working with Secretary of the Treasury John Sherman, Hayes prepared to return the United States to the gold standard, but "inflationists were shifting their support from the printing of greenbacks to the free (unlimited) coinage of silver at the ratio of 16 parts of silver to 1 part of gold. Since 1 part

Although Rutherford B. Hayes vetoed the Bland-Allison Act which created it, he requested the first struck Morgan Silver Coin for his personal collection of artifacts.

RUTHERFORD B. HAYES PRESIDENTIAL LIBRARY & MUSEUMS

of gold was worth more than 16 parts of silver, the silver coins would drive gold coins out of circulation and keep the United States off the gold standard.[5]

In 1878 Congress passed and Hayes vetoed the bipartisan Bland-Allison Act. "His concern was that the bill would negatively impact the ability of the U.S. to fulfill monetary contracts. He was alarmed that debts incurred during the time of the gold standard would be forced to accept a less valuable metal as payment. He also worried about public credit if the bill was passed. Hayes put emphasis on the reduced value of the coin, stating that the bill exaggerated the worth of the silver coins by 8 to 10 percent. Congress overrode his veto, and the Bland-Allison Act became law."[6]

In 1877, engraver George T. Morgan's design for a new silver coin won a contest at the United States Mint. "Morgan used a friend named Anna Willess Williams as his model for the Lady Liberty side of his coin. He placed an eagle on the back side that created controversy. The coin acquired the nickname of the 'buzzard dollar' because the eagle was considered scrawny. There was another issue concerning the tail feathers on the eagle. Traditionally there were seven tail feathers, but Morgan put eight on the initial design. This led to some of the original coins being collected and recast with seven feathers, although some of the coins with eight feathers remained in circulation."[7]

Although Hayes had not supported the Bland-Allison Act, he was a consummate Americana collector and expressed interest in obtaining the first-struck Morgan Silver Coin, created on March 11, 1878. It was nicknamed the "veto coin," because Hayes had voted against the legislation that created it.[8] Today the coin Hayes requested is part of the collection of the Rutherford B. Hayes Presidential Library & Museums in Fremont, Ohio.

James A. Garfield, 1881:
Inaugural Address

James A. Garfield was shot in the back by Charles Guiteau at the Baltimore and Potomac train station in Washington, D.C., on July 2, 1881, at 9:20 a.m., just a few months after his inauguration. He died on September 19, 1881, without having had a chance to make much of an impact as president. Perhaps the best object to represent him is the unfulfilled promise of his inaugural address. The original document is displayed at the James A. Garfield National Historic Site in Mentor, Ohio, alongside an invitation to his inaugural ball, which was the first event to be held at the new National Museum, today known as the Art and Industries Building at the Smithsonian.

> This was the first event held in the new building, before the exhibits were installed. A temporary wooden floor was laid for the event, two electric lights were placed in the Rotunda, 10,000 bins for hats and coats were erected, 3,000 gas lights were installed, and festive buntings, state flags and seals decorated the halls. A colossal "Statue of America" stood in the Rotunda, illustrative of peace, justice and liberty, grasping in her uplifted hand an electric light "indicative of the skill, genius, progress, and civilization" of America in the 19th century.[1]

The site was especially fitting, as Garfield had served seven terms on the Smithsonian's Board of Regents from 1865 to 1873 and 1878 to 1881. According to the Smithsonian, he was an active participant in the organization. "As a regent, Garfield was a conscientious attendee at meetings. From his letters and regular attendance, it is clear that Garfield took his duties seriously and

James Garfield's presidency was tragically cut short by an assassin's bullet. The best artifact to represent him is the unfulfilled promise of his inaugural address.

became a correspondent and colleague of both our first Secretary Joseph Henry and our second Secretary Spencer F. Baird. Garfield corresponded with Henry about a variety of subjects related to Smithsonian business, from natural history expeditions to the Smithsonian's scientific publications."[2]

Garfield's term as regent ended when he was sworn in as president, but his choice to have his inaugural ball at the new building illustrates his deep connection to the museum. "As a regent, he would have been involved in approving and monitoring the building's construction. The Board of Regents authorized its use with the condition that no precedent would be set for other uses of the building, making a special exception for the new President."[3]

Earlier in the day, Garfield had delivered his inaugural address, in which he demonstrated his strong commitment to civil rights for the formerly enslaved:

> The elevation of the negro race from slavery to the full rights of citizenship is the most important political change we have known since the adoption of the Constitution of 1787. NO thoughtful man can fail to appreciate its beneficent effect upon our institutions and people. It has freed us from the perpetual danger of war and dissolution. It has added immensely to the moral and industrial forces of our people. It has liberated the master as well as the slave from a relation which wronged and enfeebled both. It has surrendered to their own guardianship the manhood of more than 5,000,000 people, and has opened to each one of them a career of freedom and usefulness. It has given new inspiration to the power of self-help in both races by making labor more honorable to the one and more necessary to the other. The influence of this force will grow greater and bear richer fruit with the coming years.
>
> No doubt this great change has caused serious disturbance to our Southern communities. This is to be deplored, though it was perhaps unavoidable. But those who resisted the change should remember that under our institutions there was no middle ground for the negro race between slavery and equal citizenship. There can be no permanent disfranchised peasantry in the United States. Freedom can never yield its fullness of blessings so long as the law or its administration places the smallest obstacle in the pathway of any virtuous citizen.
>
> The emancipated race has already made remarkable progress. With unquestioning devotion to the Union, with a patience and gentleness not born of fear, they have "followed the light as God gave them to see the light." They are rapidly laying the material foundations of self-support, widening their circle of intelli-

gence, and beginning to enjoy the blessings that gather around the homes of the industrious poor. They deserve the generous encouragement of all good men. So far as my authority can lawfully extend they shall enjoy the full and equal protection of the Constitution and the laws.

The free enjoyment of equal suffrage is still in question, and a frank statement of the issue may aid its solution. It is alleged that in many communities negro citizens are practically denied the freedom of the ballot. In so far as the truth of this allegation is admitted, it is answered that in many places honest local government is impossible if the mass of uneducated negroes are allowed to vote. These are grave allegations. So far as the latter is true, it is the only palliation that can be offered for opposing the freedom of the ballot. Bad local government is certainly a great evil, which ought to be prevented; but to violate the freedom and sanctities of the suffrage is more than an evil. It is a crime which, if persisted in, will destroy the Government itself. Suicide is not a remedy. If in other lands it be high treason to compass the death of the king, it shall be counted no less a crime here to strangle our sovereign power and stifle its voice.[4]

Had he lived, Garfield may have been able to advance civil rights, but historians acknowledge that his options were limited. He died too soon to leave much of a legacy, which Justus Doenecke, professor emeritus of history at New College of Florida, suggests is not necessarily something negative: "For his reputation, it might have been just as well that he died when he did. He died in the prime of his life, still politically untested. The times did not demand a President in the heroic mold, and Garfield could therefore be remembered as a martyr above all else, as one who truly gave his life for his nation."[5]

21

Chester Arthur, 1881–1885: Tiffany Screen

Chester Arthur is remembered for civil service reform, reducing tariffs, and vetoing the original Chinese Exclusion Act (which he did sign when Congress reduced the 20-year immigration ban to 10 years). "Most dear to Arthur's heart as President, however, were his efforts to renovate the White House."[1] His personality was well-suited to the task:

Always known as a man of elegant taste—he is reputed to have owned eighty pairs of trousers—Arthur came to the presidency as the "Gentleman Boss." He greatly enjoyed his reputation for throwing elegant parties, for having an exquisite taste for fine food, and for socializing with the most suave and cultivated associates. Disgusted with the shabby look of the White House, he hired Louis Comfort Tiffany, the most fashionable designer in New York City, to completely refurbish the executive mansion into a showplace residence befitting the office. The price tag, funded by Congress, exceeded $30,000, which would be approximately $2 million in today's value.[2]

At the time, Tiffany was a 34-year-old painter, making a name for himself in the New York City art scene. He had recently become interested in a new way to make colored glass by mixing metal oxides into molten glass. Arthur, a fashionable widower from Manhattan, wanted to highlight the differences between himself and his predecessor, James A. Garfield, by "making the White House shine."[3] Tiffany was just the man to make that happen. He added gilded

The Grand Illumination: Sunset of the Gaslight Age, 1891. This oil painting of the Entrance Hall by Peter Waddell was made in 2006. The painting captures the lighting of a gaslight in 1891 during the Benjamin Harrison administration. The colored glass screen in the background was made by Louis Comfort Tiffany and was installed in the Entrance Hall to create a warmer welcoming for visitors while shielding the drawing rooms from the cold winter weather entering through the front door.

PETER WADELL FOR THE WHITE HOUSE HISTORICAL ASSOCIATION

tracery throughout the residence, which was designed to reflect the dancing light of the gas fixtures.

But Tiffany's most grand renovation was in the Entrance Hall. The existing glass screen, which had been installed in 1837 to block drafts, was completely transformed from a utilitarian glass wall into a dazzling stained glass showpiece in 1883. To re-create its grandeur, artist Peter Waddell researched the design in the National Archives. He was able to find most of the details he needed, except the actual colors Tiffany used. He studied other Tiffany glass designs and extrapolated the most likely color scheme from a window at Saint John's Church that Arthur had commissioned in memory of his wife, Nell.[4]

The painting itself depicts the screen in 1891, during Benjamin Harrison's administration, when the White House was converted from gas to electricity.

"Ike Hoover, electrician, has switched a wall lamp, which erupts with harsh electric light. While the new light did not impact the screen excessively, in the rooms it negated Tiffany's effects, obliterating the iridescent paint colors. Unlike the painted surfaces, which were meant to reflect and absorb light, the screen's opalescent glass was made primarily to filter light, as it does here at the end of day, when the cold, early evening light from the north is warmed to deep, rich colors, as it passes through the screen."[5]

In 1902, Teddy Roosevelt's massive classical-style renovation of the White House removed most of Arthur's Victorian-era décor, including the grand Tiffany screen.[6] It was sold as boxes of glass at auction for $275 and was partially reinstalled in the Belvedere Hotel in Chesapeake Beach, Maryland. The building was destroyed by fire in 1923.[7]

Grover Cleveland, 1885–1889 and 1893–1897: Naval Review Ribbon

When asked for a single artifact that would encompass both of Grover Cleveland's nonconsecutive terms as president, Sharon Farrell, caretaker of the Grover Cleveland Birthplace New Jersey State Historic Site, suggested this ribbon commemorating the International Naval Rendezvous and Review, which took place in Hampton Roads, Virginia, and New York Harbor in April 1893. "What was one of the most impactful accomplishments that was begun during Cleveland's first term, was still in process through his four-year gap out of the presidency, and which he was able to 'come back' and preside for at the celebration of its completion?" Farrell said. "A new Navy Fleet!"[1]

After the Civil War, our aging naval fleet was significantly inferior to other world power nations. During Cleveland's first term, Congress began authorizing the construction of one or two naval ships per year in 1886. "Grover Cleveland as a strict anti-expansionist, viewed the building up of the navy fleet as a sensible expenditure to keep the United States on par with other leading nations, especially that of Great Britain: A fleet that would be prepared to defend our interests if called for," said Farrell. "Circumstances outside of his control would eventually lead this 'New Navy' to give room for the argument of an even greater Navy and for the idea of manifest destiny and expansionism to grow. After leaving office, Cleveland would lament over the national expansionist agenda that played out before his death in 1908."[2]

In 1890, Congress directed Benjamin Harrison "to hold a naval review in New York harbor in April 1893, and to extend to foreign nations an invitation to send ships of war to join the U.S. Navy in rendezvous at Hampton Roads and proceed thence to said review."[3] At least 20 nations were invited to participate, but some, including China, Turkey, and Uruguay, had to decline since they did not have any ships available. "For those countries that did accept, the selection of which warships to send became a delicate diplomatic juggling act. When Russia announced it would send five vessels, England promptly added HMS *Australia* from the Mediterranean station to bring its representation to the same number."[4]

On the day of the event, nine nations participated in front of large crowds:

By the 17th, Hampton Roads began to fill as the British squadron of five ships were joined that afternoon by Dutch and French vessels. Warships would continue to trickle in over the next week. Some that were expected did not show. Three Russian cruisers were prevented from attending by ice in the Baltic. The Argentine protected cruiser *Nueve de Julio* simply bypassed the Virginia affair and headed straight for New York. But to the immense crowds of onlookers these absentees were unimportant. The population of the cities surrounding the Roads swelled by 50,000. Prices soared. "It costs 30 cents to get shaved, and only the wealthiest are able to afford a hair-cut," lamented the Virginian.

This commemorative ribbon was worn by President Grover Cleveland at the International Naval Rendezvous and Review in 1893. It is engraved with his name at the top.

COLLECTION OF THE GROVER CLEVELAND BIRTHPLACE NEW JERSEY STATE HISTORIC SITE, GIFT OF RICHARD F. CLEVELAND, SON OF GROVER CLEVELAND, 1950.

Local watermen made small fortunes charging $5 an hour to ferry sight-seers amongst the anchored warships. The Hygeia Hotel at Old Point Comfort turned away enough people to have doubled its occupancy daily. Even bad weather in mid-week could not dampen the crowd's spirits. In the face of high winds, ladies simply sewed lead shot in the hems of their skirts to prevent "an undue display of ankles as they clambered up the steep landing steps of the ships."[5]

President Cleveland attended the review aboard the USS *Dolphin*. According to the secretary of the navy's report on the day, the weather was fine, and the ships were impressive: "As the '*Dolphin*' hove in sight there was not a cloud in the sky, and each of the thirty war-ships in view seemed hung with rainbows of many colors. They were all dressed in the gay colors of Italy in honor of the twenty-fifth anniversary of King Humbert's marriage."[6]

In his first annual message of his second term, given on December 4, 1893, Cleveland provided an update on the status of the navy, outlining why it was still important to continue to invest resources into shipbuilding:

> The report of the Secretary of the Navy contains a history of the operations of his Department during the past year and exhibits a most gratifying condition of the personnel of our Navy. He presents a satisfactory account of the progress which has been made in the construction of vessels and makes a number of recommendations to which attention is especially invited.
>
> During the past six months the demands for cruising vessels have been many and urgent. There have been revolutions calling for vessels to protect American interests in Nicaragua, Guatemala, Costa Rica, Honduras, Argentina, and Brazil, while the condition of affairs in Honolulu has required the constant presence of one or more ships. With all these calls upon our Navy it became necessary, in order to make up a sufficient fleet to patrol the Bering Sea under the modus vivendi agreed upon with Great Britain, to detail to that service one vessel from the Fish Commission and three from the Revenue Marine.[7]

In spite of some construction delays, Cleveland announced that the following ships where ready for service: the double-turreted coast-defense monitors *Miantonomoh* and *Monterey*; armored cruiser *New York*; protected cruisers *Baltimore, Chicago, Philadelphia, Newark, San Francisco, Charleston, Atlanta,* and *Boston*; gunboats *Yorktown, Concord, Bennington, Machias, Castine,* and *Petrel*; dispatch vessel *Dolphin*; practice vessel *Bancroft*; and dynamite gunboat *Vesuvius*. He reported that several other ships were currently under construction and were expected to be completed by 1896.

Benjamin Harrison, 1889–1893: *Judge* Cartoon

Since more states joined the Union under Benjamin Harrison's administration than any other president, the staff at the Benjamin Harrison Presidential Site thought this *Judge* cartoon best captured his legacy. New states included North Dakota and South Dakota (November 2, 1889), Montana (November 8, 1889), Washington (November 11, 1889), Idaho (July 3, 1890), and Wyoming (July 10, 1890). The cartoon's caption reads:

> The Republican Party's First Duty—
> The Introduction of Dakota
> B. Harrison
> "Miss Dakota, you have been kept out by
> Democratic prejudice long enough—
> Pray, join your sisters!"

In addition to adding 12 new senators and 18 new electors to the Electoral College,[1] the impact of admitting these states would be far-reaching:

The new states impacted American politics by focusing political attention on western issues like never before. Located far from the eastern United States, the new West at the turn of the century would demand government support for transforming the landscape. Mesas, buttes, dry terrain, and vast grasslands were turned into ranches, farms, mines, timber factories, fisheries, and vacation resorts. The new communities of the West would also need infrastructure for basic needs such as commerce, transportation, communication, water, and power. Thus, the government would become involved in giving land to railroad and telegraph companies, constructing dams and irrigation canals, and providing mining concessions.[2]

Adding new states was also part of a larger political strategy for the Republicans, which was no secret in Washington. "Republicans did not hide their intentions," said Heather Cox Richardson, writing for *The Atlantic*. "In the popular *Frank Leslie's Illustrated Newspaper*, President Harrison's son crowed that the Republicans would win all the new states and gain eight more senators, while the states' new electors meant that Cleveland's New York would no longer dominate the Electoral College. When the Republicans' popularity continued to fall nationally, in 1890 Congress added Wyoming and Idaho—whose populations in 1880 were fewer than 21,000 and 33,000 respectively—organizing them so quickly that they bypassed normal procedures and permitted volunteers instead of elected delegates to write Idaho's constitution."[3]

Judge cartoon, 1889, showing Harrison introducing Dakota (a lady carrying wheat) to a crowd of ladies that represent the other states in the Union, including Ohio, Indiana, New York, Maine, and Oregon.

BENJAMIN HARRISON PRESIDENTIAL SITE

Less populous states received disproportionate representation in Congress and the Electoral College, sparking debates that echo modern criticism about how governmental power is distributed. Adding Republican-leaning states to the Union would obviously benefit the Republican Party. With a Republican winner declared in the election of 1888, Democrat Grover Cleveland signed an act before leaving office that divided the Dakota Territory in half and allowed Montana and Washington to write constitutions in preparation for becoming states. The northern and southern regions of Dakota were developing distinctly different personalities, and dividing it would be advantageous for the Democrats. The statehood plan completely overlooked New Mexico, the other Democratic choice, which had twice as many people as any of the other proposed states. The Dakotas were admitted on the same day, but no one knows which one was first. Harrison reportedly shuffled the paperwork and signed both of them without looking at what the papers said.[4] Montana and Washington were added, separately, a few days later.

Moderate Republicans sided with the Democrats, "pointing out that the Harrison administration had badly undercut the political power of voters from populous regions, attacking America's fundamental principle of equal representation." Sparsely populated states like Wyoming and Idaho would have four senators and two representatives, even though there were "fewer people in both together than in some of Massachusetts's congressional districts."[5]

The authority to admit a new state is outlined in Article IV, Section III of the US Constitution:

> New States may be admitted by the Congress into this Union; but no new State shall be formed or erected within the Jurisdiction of any other State; nor any State be formed by the Junction of two or more States, or Parts of States, without the Consent of the Legislatures of the States concerned as well as of the Congress.[6]

Most of the debate at the Constitutional Convention focused on the last part, which requires the consent of an existing state if a new state is to be created from within its borders. Although the Constitution is clear about who can admit a state, it says almost nothing about the process that should be followed. Typically a territorial government was established first through an Enabling Act, which also authorized the territory to draft a state constitution in order to apply for statehood. There has never been a uniform set of conditions.

Often in the Enabling Act, Congress specified a range of conditions that the proposed state had to meet in order for admission to occur. These conditions varied widely across time and states. For example, some states were precluded from allowing polygamy or slavery, and some states were forced to practice religious toleration or to afford civil jury trial rights.[7]

Sometimes the Enabling Act delegated the final approval process to the president, which is why Harrison signed the documents for the states admitted under his administration.

William McKinley, 1897–1901: McKinley National Memorial Collection Bank

When the news broke that President William McKinley had been shot on September 6, 1901 at the Temple of Music of the Pan-American Exposition in Buffalo, New York, it marked the third time in just 36 years that a US president had been shot. An adult who was roughly 40 years old at the time would have remembered each assassination. And yet, no formal protection existed to help prevent such tragedies.

When assassin Leon Czolgosz shot him at close range, McKinley was just six months into his second term. A popular public figure, he had soundly defeated Democrat William Jennings Bryan in both the 1896 and 1900 elections, winning by an even greater margin the second time. The economy was already starting to improve when he took office, but he also inherited ongoing tensions between Cuba and Spain. After the USS *Maine* exploded in Havana Harbor on February 15, 1898, Congress declared war in April. Americans enthusiastically supported the Spanish-American War, with some even equating it to the excitement of a major sporting event. The war was brief, and although 5,462 men lost their lives, the American victory was decisive, largely due to the decision to modernize the US Navy earlier in the 1890s.[1]

Alongside its declaration of war, Congress had also authorized the Secret Service to protect the president, but only for the duration of the war. Today its mission to provide security to the president, vice president, and their families is widely understood, but the Secret Service was actually created during the Civil War to combat counterfeit currency. Protecting the president was a side job that began in 1894 when Chief William P. Hazen used the wider scope declared by Congress in 1867 to "detect persons perpetuating frauds against the government" as the justification to assign two guards to protect President Grover Cleveland. Technically Hazen was not authorized to provide such a service, but he argued that it was justified because agents had uncovered a plot to kill Garfield while investigating a possible gambling ring.[2]

The Secret Service agents continued their clandestine assignment after McKinley's inauguration in March 1897, but during a routine audit by the Treasury Department, Hazen's brash expansion of his organization's role was discovered. For his "shocking administrative mismanagement," Hazen was demoted to a field operative and replaced by John E. Wilkie, a friend of McKinley's and a former journalist for the *Chicago Tribune*.[3]

When Congress authorized Secret Service protection for McKinley in 1898, it provided four agents for the duration of the war only. After that, the Washington, D.C., metropolitan police provided security, although the Secret Service was present when the president traveled. On that fateful trip to Buffalo, McKinley decided to greet the public on "President's Day" at the Pan-American Exposition. He was accompanied by George Foster, his regular security guard outside of Washington, D.C., Secret Service agents Samuel Ireland and Albert

The entire nation mourned William McKinley's tragic death in 1901. The McKinley National Memorial Association distributed banks like these to collect money to build a suitable memorial to the slain president.

MCKINLEY PRESIDENTIAL LIBRARY & MUSEUM

Gallagher, and members of the local police department. McKinley shook hands with each person in the long line. In his article "The Assassination of President William McKinley: A Catalyst for Change in Protecting the President," Christopher Kenney described what happened next: "According to eyewitnesses, a man shook hands longer than many thought necessary, drawing attention to himself. Guards, as if by rote, quickly moved him along, and during this commotion they failed to notice the next man in line with a handkerchief wrapped around his hand. The man was Leon Czolgosz, an anarchist who viewed the office of presidency as a threat to the workingman." Czolgosz shot the president twice before being tackled. McKinley would die eight days later, on September 14, 1901. Justice was swift. Czolgosz, who had immediately confessed to the murder in police custody without knowing that McKinley was still alive, was executed by electric chair on October 29, 1901 at Auburn Prison in Auburn, New York.[4]

On the day of his funeral, McKinley's closest friends and advisors met to discuss a suitable memorial to the slain president. They chose a site that McKinley had often visited when he was at home in Canton, Ohio. "He admired the sweeping view and remarked that it would be a proper site for a monument—not for him, but for the soldiers and sailors from Stark County who had given their lives during times of war," Kenney wrote.[5] This group of men became the McKinley National Memorial Association, charged with raising the funds, selecting the design, and overseeing the construction of a monument to their friend and colleague. Estimating it would need to raise $600,000, they issued a public appeal for donations on October 10, 1901.

Fundraising would be a national undertaking. According to Kenney, "Committees were set up in each state to coordinate the fundraising efforts. Each state in the Union was assigned a monetary amount to collect determined by its population. The American Bankers Association designated all banks as donation sites, and all postal carriers were instructed to accept donations. To offset the cost of sending official telegraphs, Western Union and Postal Telegraph each credited the association with $2,500. In Canton, the Association placed small metal banks throughout the community to collect spare change." The McKinley Presidential Library & Museum has two of these banks in its permanent collection.

Once enough funds had been raised to purchase land, the Association acquired 26 acres from West Lawn Cemetery. A national design competition resulted in submissions ranging from massive, sprawling structures to more modest mausoleums that might be found in a typical cemetery setting. Ultimately the committee chose architect Harold Van Buren Magonigle's design, influenced by Greek revival or neo-Classical style. Each detail was specifically chosen to tell the story of McKinley's life. The McKinley National Memorial stands at the top of 108 steps. Half way up is a bronze statue, sculpted by Charles Henry Niehaus from a photograph of McKinley giving his final speech in Buffalo shortly before he was shot. The Memorial itself features the largest brass doors ever cast at the time, situated beneath an exterior lunette that is an allegory depicting War laying his sword at the feet of the Republic on one side and Industry presenting her with the fruits of his labor on the other. The marble double sarcophagus inside the Memorial was deliberately raised so visitors would need to look up in reverence to the president and first lady. The couple's two young daughters are buried inside the Memorial's northern wall.

An aerial view of the property reveals more details about the design. According to Kenney, "Magonigle envisioned the monument at the center of a large cross, representing the cross of a martyred president. . . . That cross would also form the handle of a sword, symbolizing McKinley's military career and his role as commander in chief during the Spanish-American War. The blade of the sword was formed by what was called the Long Water, a 575-foot lagoon made up of five different levels, each twenty inches higher than the one before. The water cascaded down and ended in a reflecting pond."

As fundraising and construction of the McKinley National Memorial was taking place, the public and government officials alike struggled to understand how this assassination happened and what could have been done to prevent it. "It was clear changes needed to be made," Kenney wrote. "Although the Secret Service still had no official authorization to provide presidential protection, Director Wilkie immediately stationed two agents at the White House full-time to protect President Roosevelt and his family. Congress wanted official protection for the president but struggled with how to best achieve that goal."[6]

Although several bills were proposed, none of them passed. One idea was to use Army soldiers for security, since they would already be trained. This measure ultimately failed because Congress was "traditionally reluctant to elevate the entourage of the presidency to the status of a monarchy. Unfettered access to the nation's chief executive had been a hallmark of American democracy, setting it apart from European nations whose rulers were secreted away in palaces with limited exposure to their subjects. But with three assassinations in less than forty years, Congress needed to reevaluate its stance on presidential protection."[7]

As the debate continued, George Cortelyou, the president's personal secretary, called a meeting at his home on October 4, 1901, specifically to discuss the protection of the president. Earlier that day, Cortelyou had spoken to President Theodore Roosevelt regarding this issue. At first Roosevelt did not see the importance of full-time protection, but in the same conversation, he changed his mind and asked Cortelyou to "do whatever he thought best in this direction." Present at this meeting were Major Richard Sylvester, superintendent of police for Washington, D.C.; W. E. Cochran, chief post office inspector; and W. H. Moran, chief clerk of the Secret Service. Cortelyou envisioned a solution where all three organizations would "act in perfect concert at all times in this work."[8]

In spite of all the discussions that took place in the days after McKinley's assassination, Congress would not be able to agree on a course of action until the Sundry Civil Expenses Act of 1907, which officially allocated funds for the protection of the president by the Secret Service in the same year that the McKinley National Memorial was completed and dedicated. As part of McKinley's legacy, every American president since Teddy Roosevelt has received full-time Secret Service protection. The mission of the Secret Service has continued to evolve. "In the 21st century, the Secret Service's duty to protect the president has become more complex," Kenney wrote, "with threats coming in ways that President McKinley could never have imagined."[9]

Theodore Roosevelt, 1901–1909: Page from Speech

After William McKinley was assassinated in 1901, the nation's new president could not have been more different from his predecessor. McKinley was mild mannered and steadfast, the last president to serve in the Victorian era. By contrast, Theodore Roosevelt was larger than life, and nothing illustrates that better than the fact that he continued to deliver a speech after being shot.

After his second term, the first one for which he was elected, Roosevelt announced that he would not run again. Although there were no term limits in place yet, when he was elected on his own in 1904, he promised not to seek reelection for a third term and hand-picked William Howard Taft as his successor.

Originally Taft had agreed to keep most of Roosevelt's cabinet members, but he soon discovered that having his own choices in those roles would suit him better. Roosevelt was annoyed that Taft did not consult him, and soon after the inauguration, he left on a trip throughout Africa and Europe that lasted more than a year. While he was out of the country, old friends kept him informed about what was going on in Taft's administration, and most of what he heard displeased him.

Under pressure from the progressive faction of the Republican Party, Roosevelt agreed to challenge Taft in 1912. After failing to win the nomination at the convention, he and his supporters formed their own third party. Officially known as the National Progressive Party, its popular name became the Bull Moose Party when Roosevelt said he felt "as strong as a bull moose" in a speech. His platform was consistent with the progressive issues he had championed as president:

> Its tenets included political justice and economic opportunity, and it sought a minimum wage for women; an eight-hour workday; a social security system; a national health service; a federal securities commission; and direct election of U.S. senators. The platform also supported the initiative, referendum, and recall as means for the people to exert more direct control over government. TR worried about the power of the minority—often politicians—over the majority and thought these changes would make government more accountable to the people.[1]

Roosevelt threw himself into his campaign, visiting 38 states to deliver speeches to adoring crowds.

On October 14, 1912, Roosevelt was in Milwaukee, Wisconsin, to give his third campaign speech of the day. His voice was growing hoarse, but he seemed to possess unlimited energy for campaigning. He opened his speech with a line no one expected: "Friends, I shall ask you to be as quiet as possible," he said. "I don't know whether you fully understand that I have just been shot."[2] The assassin, John Schrank, had shot him outside of the Hotel Gilpatrick as he was leaving for the auditorium where he was scheduled to speak. Schrank believed that he was "acting on orders from the ghost of President William McKinley."[3] From his military training and experience as a cowboy and big game hunter, Roosevelt instinctively coughed into his hand to check for blood. Finding none, he knew that his lungs were not injured, and he insisted on continuing on to the auditorium as planned. Backstage, doctors confirmed that the injuries were not life-threatening, and he proceeded to the stage.[4]

Fortunately for Roosevelt, his 50-page speech had been folded in his heavy overcoat pocket, next to his steel-reinforced eyeglass case, which together worked to slow the bullet enough that it did not kill him. In true Roosevelt fashion, he refused to be taken to the hospital until he finished his speech. "It takes more than that to kill a bull moose," he said. "Fortunately I had my manuscript, so you see I was going to make a long speech, and there is a bullet—there is where the bullet went through—and it probably saved me from it going into my heart. The bullet is in me now, so that I cannot make a very long speech, but I will try my best."[5] Aides urged him to stop at several points, but he continued to speak for over an hour.

Although Roosevelt did not go on to win the election, he did very well for a third-party candidate, capturing 27.4 percent of the vote. The steely nerve displayed during his assassination attempt no doubt won him votes. "Roosevelt's courageous—perhaps foolhardy—act reminded Americans of what they loved about him," said Sidney Milkis, professor of politics at the University of Virginia.[6]

So what happened to the pages of his famous bullet-ridden speech? Patricia O'Toole writes, "As he continued, TR followed his practice of dropping each page when he finished reading it. Journalists often took a leaf or two as souvenirs; on this occasion, Samuel Marrs, a Chicago photographer, scooped up the bullet-pierced page seen here."[7] The Smithsonian acquired it from Marrs's nephew in 1974.

The pages of his lengthy speech saved Theodore Roosevelt from a would-be assassin's bullet during a campaign stop in 1912.

PHOTO BY CADE MARTIN

William Howard Taft, 1909–1913: Bible

William Howard Taft remains the only person to have served as both president of the United States and Supreme Court justice. According to his obituary in the *New York Times*, he was much better suited to the latter: "His appointment by President Harding as Chief Justice of the Supreme Court of the United States, an office which by both temperament and training he was better fitted to hold than that of President, came as a realization of a lifelong ambition, and was received with every manifestation of popular approval. It was a 'come-back' unprecedented in American political annals."[1]

Back in 1900, Taft had shared his ambition to become a Supreme Court justice with William McKinley, who appointed him chairman of a commission to create a government in the Philippines following the Spanish-American War. Taft served as secretary of war under Theodore Roosevelt, who later handpicked him as his successor for the Republican Party's nomination in 1908. Throughout his career he was often conflicted between continuing in politics or pursuing a judicial position. Roosevelt offered him a Supreme Court seat, but ultimately convinced him that the presidency would be easily won, so he agreed to run.

Although Taft's résumé was filled with significant and valuable experience, most of it had not been political:

> After he was installed in the White House many of his most loyal friends realized that perhaps his training had not been altogether of the right sort, from a political point of view. Mr. Taft had not been reared in the school of practical

politics. He had not rubbed elbows with the party workers or fought his way up through the party ranks. Consequently, they felt, he lacked that keen insight into the motives and methods of practical politicians which many of his predecessors had possessed and used with effectiveness. . . . Mr. Taft often said himself that he felt a lack of that character of political training which would have thrown him into closer contact with the masses of the people. He had never been district leader, Alderman, Mayor or legislator. His training had been judicial and his circle of contact small.[2]

Shortly after his election, Taft and Roosevelt had a falling out, which ultimately cost them both reelection when Roosevelt split the Republican vote in 1912. The two reportedly reconciled before Roosevelt's death. After losing the election, Taft became a professor of law at Yale University and was elected president of the American Bar Association.

William Howard Taft used this Bible when he was sworn in as both president of the United States and chief justice of the Supreme Court.

WILLIAM HOWARD TAFT NATIONAL HISTORIC SITE

While he was president, Taft had appointed six of the nine Supreme Court justices. When the time was finally right, Taft accepted his own nomination, but insisted that he would only accept the position of chief justice, since he had nominated so many of the men who sat on the court.[3] He was sworn in, using the same Bible he had used at his presidential inauguration, on July 11, 1921.

Taft was an active justice, writing more than 250 mostly conservative opinions between 1921 and 1930. By all accounts, he was much happier in his role as chief justice than he had ever been as president. It was a world he understood, and he excelled at his position. In the *Smithsonian* magazine, "Justice Sandra Day O'Connor called Taft a 'great Chief Justice . . . who deserves almost as much credit as [John] Marshall for the Court's modern-day role but who does not often receive the recognition.' She noted that 84 percent of the Taft court's opinions were unanimous—a reflection of his attempts to craft opinions that kept the nine justices together. 'Most dissents,' Taft said, 'are a form of egotism. They don't do any good, and only weaken the prestige of the court.'"[4]

Taft reluctantly stepped down for health reasons on February 3, 1930. He died a month later, from complications from heart disease, high blood pressure, and bladder inflammation.

Woodrow Wilson, 1913–1921: 1919 Pierce-Arrow

Wilson first rode in this 1919 Pierce-Arrow on July 9, 1919, when it picked him up at Union Station in Washington, D.C., after the last leg of his return trip from the Paris Peace Conference. "It quickly became his preferred car in the White House fleet," said Andrew R. Phillips, curator and director of museum operations at the Woodrow Wilson Presidential Library. "Wilson loved cars, though we have no evidence he ever had a driver's license. He was a member of AAA and the symbol of the organization was placed on the grill." Its "presidential" features are only decorative, as it does not have any of the safety features, such as extra thick walls and bulletproof glass, that we have come to expect of a modern presidential vehicle.[1]

A year before the conference, Wilson had debuted his vision for peace after World War I on January 8, 1918, when he delivered his "Fourteen Points" speech to Congress. His recommendations called for an end to secret alliances that had pulled many countries into the war, evacuation of all occupied territories, and general disarmament. But the issue that was most important to Wilson was the League of Nations, which he believed would prevent future wars. According to Saladin Ambar, associate professor of political science at Rutgers University–New Brunswick, "This new world body would be in charge of disarmament and the dismantling of colonial possessions. Most importantly, the League would hold power over all disputes among its members. Wilson believed that this League would transform international relations and usher in a new era of world peace."[2]

Wilson led the American delegation of the Paris Peace Conference, which began in January 1919 and went for about six months. Wilson was in Europe for most of that time, returning home for a just a few weeks in February. He toured France, Britain, and Italy, where he was greeted warmly by the public. Wilson understood that his ideas were not popular with national leaders, but he hoped if he could convince the people themselves, their leaders would follow. He underestimated the appetite for vengeance against Germany.

In the end, Wilson was forced to compromise many of his points, and the resulting Treaty of Versailles reflects "strict punitive measures" for Germany, such as surrendering all of its overseas possessions and 10 percent of its prewar territory in Europe; limiting the size of its Army and Navy; accepting responsibility for the war; and agreeing to pay reparations to the Allies.[3] The treaty was signed on June 28, and Wilson set sail for home the next day aboard the SS *George Washington*. He arrived in Hoboken, New Jersey, on July 8 and

1919 Series 51 Pierce-Arrow limousine, made in Buffalo, New York, and leased to the government for use at the White House in June 1919. This model cost $9,250 and was the top of the line for an American automobile, including an electric starter, intercom system, and seating for five in the passenger compartment. It features an eagle and union shield radiator cap, flag holders on the front bumper, and the seal of the president on the passenger doors.

took a train to Washington, D.C., where the Pierce-Arrow picked him up and drove him to the White House.[4]

Much to his disappointment, Wilson was not able to gain enough support in Congress to ratify the treaty. Most of the opposition was against the League of Nations. The United States signed a separate treaty with Germany in August instead.

A few months later, Wilson suffered a serious stroke that left him debilitated for the rest of his life. "This was the period in which his wife, Edith Bolling Galt Wilson, his doctor, Cary T. Grayson, and his secretary, Joseph Tumulty, conspired to prevent the severity of his condition from getting out to the press, American public, or other members of the executive branch," said Phillips. "He would be able to walk again, but was frail and tired easily and had to give up many of his more active leisure activities. One of the few outdoor activities he could still enjoy was car rides."[5]

After Wilson left office in 1921, friends purchased the car as a gift for him. "To mark its transition to a civilian vehicle, decorative changes were made, including orange pinstriping (for Princeton University) and the presidential seal was replaced with a silver WW," said Phillips. "It would be Wilson's primary transportation in the last few years of his life, while living on S Street in Washington, D.C., and he continued his new tradition of almost daily car rides around the city. An avid baseball fan, Wilson attended the occasional Washington Senators game, but because of his infirmity, he was not able to negotiate the grandstands. Instead, the car would be parked in the outfield (behind the foul line) and a player would be posted to sit on the front bumper, ensuring no errant foul balls hit the former president's car."[6]

After Wilson's death in February 1924, his widow, Edith, donated the car to "leading citizens of Staunton" in 1925, with the understanding that it would be included in a planned shrine to her late husband. The car was the first item in the collection of the Woodrow Wilson Birthplace Foundation, which is now the Woodrow Wilson Presidential Library. "It has always been in working order," said Phillips, "though sometimes working better than others, and it is the oldest operational presidential car in the country."[7]

28

Warren G. Harding, 1921–1923: Skeleton Key

Sometimes the artifact that best represents a president isn't presidential at all.

For nearly four decades, Harding carried this folding skeleton key in his pocket. In his foreword to Sherry Hall's book on Harding and the *Marion Star*, Edward Looman, former managing editor of the *Marion Star*, quoted her in a speech she gave in 2013: "There is a long well-worn skeleton key on Mr. Harding's desk in the Harding Home. It's no secret to my co-workers that the key is one of my favorite objects in the house. That key unlocked the front door of the *Marion Star* office building on Center Street. Mr. Harding carried that old key in his pocket for almost forty years, including while he was president. The key says it all about President Harding."[1] Although he admitted he was probably in over his head shortly after his election, Harding brought his love of his hometown, his state, and his country with him to Washington. Sadly, that just wasn't enough to make him a successful president.

Warren G. Harding described himself as a newspaper man through and through, as author Sherry Hall explains, "His newspaper, the *Marion Daily Star* in Marion, Ohio, had been his constant companion for all of his adult years—almost a living, breathing being in his eyes, a project that he had nursed from its infancy. It was the anchor that kept him grounded through his political career. It would do the same for him during his presidency."[2] This key unlocked the front door to his newspaper building, which was closer to his heart than the office he occupied in the White House.

Harding had purchased the struggling newspaper back in 1884 after try-ing several different careers, including teaching in a one-room schoolhouse and selling insurance. "Only the pungent odor of printer's ink and the feel of soft, white newsprint made his blood race," wrote Hall.[3] Harding was the face of his newspaper from the beginning, which was greeted with skepticism by the people of Marion. There were already two other newspapers in the small town, and Harding and his business associates were young and new to the newspaper business. Money was tight in those early days, and Harding and his business partner often sacrificed their own salaries to pay their staff. Still, Harding threw himself into his newspaper, and eventually his hard work paid off.

Harding began to build his future political career by joining almost every fraternal organization in town. He was invited to many events and parties, which he often wrote about in great detail in the next day's edition. He did not shy away from political or controversial topics, writing about such issues as prohibition and unregulated immigration. By the election of 1896, Hard-ing had established himself as an up-and-coming member of the Republican Party and was asked to travel throughout Ohio to give speeches on behalf of William McKinley. In 1899 he was elected to the State Senate, serving two terms. The key to his success in those early years was his "ability to work with senators of both parties and to weave solutions to seeming impasses, which left each party saving face."[4] Harding served as lieutenant governor from 1904 to 1906, and he established a lucrative speaking career in addition to his suc-cess with the *Star*. After losing the gubernatorial race in 1910, he returned his full attention to his newspaper, but politics continued to call to him. In 1914 Harding was elected to the US Senate. Although he and his wife moved to Washington, D.C., he spent much of his time running the *Star* from a distance. Whenever he returned to Marion, he immersed himself in his newspaper work, which gave him more joy than anything else in his life.

Running for president was not part of Harding's plan. He was content in the Senate, but pressure from friends and colleagues led to his nomination in 1920. In short order, he announced his plans to run a front-porch campaign from Marion, as McKinley had done in Canton in 1896. His popularity in his hometown fueled the success of his presidential aspirations. From his porch, Harding shared his plans with more than six hundred thousand people who came to town to hear him speak. "His 'Return to Normlacy' campaign slogan promised a common-sense approach to returning the nation to balance after America's preoccupation with the Great War."[5] Harding's easy manner with other reporters made his informal press conferences successful. He wrote most of his speeches himself, scrawling his words in pencil on a pad of paper. He easily won the election against fellow newspaperman and governor of Ohio James M. Cox with over 60 percent of the popular vote.

Throughout his presidency, issues of the *Star* were delivered by mail to the White House, and his many years as a journalist informed his work as chief executive. "Warren Harding the president used much of the same reasoning to address issues as had Warren Harding the small-town publisher," wrote Hall. "The ups and downs of building the *Star* were rooted in him so deeply that he could not do otherwise."[6] After serving as president, Harding intended to retire from active ownership of the *Star* but remain as an editorial writer, which no former president had done before. In 1923 he sold the *Star* to Roy Moore and Louis Brush, who would go on to create the conglomerate Brush-Moore Newspapers. A few months later, while on an extensive presidential tour of the western states, Harding suffered a heart attack and died on August 2, 1923.

This skeleton key opened the front door of Warren G. Harding's beloved *Marion Daily Star* in Marion, Ohio.
WARREN G. HARDING PRESIDENTIAL SITES

29

Calvin Coolidge, 1923–1929: Painting of Inauguration

After the sudden death of Warren G. Harding, Calvin Coolidge was sworn in as president of the United States in the middle of the night on August 3, 1923. This painting depicts what became known as the "Homestead Inaugural." In his autobiography, published in 1929, Coolidge wrote, "The picture of this scene has been painted with historical accuracy by an artist named Keller, who went to Plymouth for that purpose. Although the likenesses are not good, everything in relation to the painting is correct."[1] After the ceremony, which was performed by his father, Coolidge reportedly went back to bed.

Coolidge grew up in the town of Plymouth Notch, Vermont, a small village that looks very much as it did when he lived there. Many of the historic buildings, including the homes of the Coolidge family, the community church, and a one-room schoolhouse, have been preserved as the "Plymouth Notch Historic District" and is owned and operated by the Vermont Division for Historic Preservation.

Vice President Coolidge was on vacation at the family home when word arrived of Harding's death. "A telephone call placed from the general store to Washington, D.C., confirmed that Colonel John Coolidge, as a notary public, had sufficient authority to administer the Presidential Oath of Office," William W. Jenney, Regional Historic Site administrator of the President Calvin Coolidge State Historic Site. "Thus, Colonel John swore in his son as president in the sitting room. The event, unique in American history, occurred on August 3 at 2:47 a.m. by the light of a kerosene lamp. Coolidge recorded that Grace Coolidge (his wife), Porter H. Dale (soon to be US Senator from

The Swearing in of Calvin Coolidge by His Father, Arthur I. Keller, oil on canvas, circa 1923.
VERMONT DIVISION FOR HISTORIC PRESERVATION, PRESIDENT CALVIN COOLIDGE STATE HISTORIC SITE

Vermont), Erwin C. Geisser (Coolidge's stenographer), and Joseph McInerney (Coolidge's chauffeur) were also in attendance." Coolidge, who was known as "Silent Cal" for his quiet and cool demeanor, would later write, "It seemed a simple and natural thing to do at the time, but I can now realize something of the dramatic force of the event."[2]

Coolidge's approach to governing is best described as "passive." Although he was highly visible in the media, he believed in small government with little interference from the executive branch, if he could help it. He enjoyed a favorable public opinion for most of his administration, but in August 1927 he issued a one-sentence statement that he would not be seeking reelection in 1928.

Today, almost nothing has changed in the home where Coolidge became president. According to Jenney, "Colonel John Coolidge lived in Homestead until his death in 1926. His housekeeper, Aurora Pierce, stayed on for another 30 years. Aurora never accepted the easy life of electricity and 'new-fangled' plumbing, and the house remained much as it was in 1923. An addition built by the president in 1931 was removed in 1956 when the president's son and daughter-in-law, John and Florence, gave the house and its contents to the State of Vermont. The rooms are furnished exactly as they were in 1923; the kerosene lamp, family Bible, and pearl-handled pen that was used to sign the three copies of the oath of office are still on the center table in the sitting room."[3]

30

Herbert Hoover, 1929–1933: Humidor

Herbert Hoover had the dubious honor of presiding over the country when the stock market crashed and the economy spiraled into the Great Depression. With the stress of the job under such conditions, Hoover must have been grateful for the creation of his informal "medicine ball cabinet" at the beginning of his presidency.

On March 4, 1929, following his inauguration, Hoover met with White House physician Dr. Joel T. Boone for a physical. Although the president was in relatively good health, the doctor noted that his blood pressure was "not as strong as expected" and he needed to lose 25 pounds. He suggested going on a diet and getting some exercise out in the fresh air.[1]

Hoover understood it was no small task to schedule a regular fitness routine as president of the United States. In his memoirs he wrote, "Getting daily exercise to keep physically fit is always a problem for Presidents. Once the day's work starts there is little chance to walk, to ride or to take part in a game."[2] With limited time for exercise, Hoover wanted an activity that would stimulate his mind as well as his body, so Dr. Boone suggested throwing an eight-pound medicine ball back and forth. What he had in mind was not a simple game of catch, but rather a new game altogether. It would eventually become known as Hoover Ball.

On the decks of battleships, sailors often used a medicine ball to play a game called "bull in the ring," which was more like "keep away" than Boone's creation. It took him several months to establish the rules for the game, which is a combination of medicine ball, volleyball, and tennis. In his article "Hoover Ball and Wellness in the White House," Matthew Schaefer explains the game:

The official court is 66 by 30 feet. The ball is to weigh 4 to 6 pounds. This contrasts with a volleyball, which weighs less than 10 ounces. The Hoover Ball consists of a hand-stitched leather cover around a sandbag core wrapped in cotton batting. The net is to be 8 feet high. Teams consist of two to four players. Scoring is exactly like tennis: love, 15, 30, 40 (deuce, ad-in, ad-out), game. Teams play matches of best of five or seven games. Points are scored when a team fails to catch the ball, fails to return the ball across the net, returns the ball out-of-bounds, or fails to return the ball to the proper court area. Points in question are played over. Good sportsmanship is expected. The ball is served from the back line. . . . The ball must be caught on the fly and returned from the point it was caught. There is no running with the ball or passing it to teammates. . . . Balls caught must be played.[3]

This silver humidor depicts Herbert Hoover's famous "Medicine Ball Cabinet," with whom he regularly exercised and de-stressed.
NATIONAL ARCHIVES, HERBERT HOOVER PRESIDENTIAL LIBRARY-MUSEUM

Hoover's first "medicine ball cabinet" included Larry Richey, his personal secretary; Dr. Boone; Ray Lyman Wilbur, secretary of the interior; Arthur Hyde, secretary of agriculture; and Supreme Court Justice Harlan Stone. Hoover began playing six days a week with a variety of men who "wanted face-time with the president."[4]

Soon the press began to cover the new phenomenon taking place on the south lawn of the White House. On March 25, 1929, the *News-Journal* in Mansfield wrote, "Harding golfed, Coolidge walked and rode a mechanical horse, but President Hoover tosses the medicine ball each morning to get his daily exercise. What might be called White House medicine ball club meets each morning at the White House at seven o'clock. . . . They toss the ball around in the south grounds for a brisk half hour and then go to breakfast."[5]

This daily ritual was not only beneficial for Hoover's physical health, it was also an important stress reliever as well. The game allowed him to step back from the White House and relax, while bouncing ideas around with his closest friends and advisors. As Dr. Boone put it, Hoover could forget he was president for 30 minutes a day. "Mr. Hoover is not permitted to think about anything but the six pound ball hurtling toward him," he wrote.[6]

And Hoover had plenty to worry about.

Before becoming president, Hoover had distinguished himself as a humanitarian. He assisted Americans trying to return from Europe at the outbreak of World War I, distributed food in Belgium after German occupation, helped direct aid to the victims of the Great Mississippi Flood of 1927, and created the concept of the long-term mortgage to expand homeownership. He was seen as a "man of the people" when he easily won his election in 1928.[7]

Everything changed when the stock market crashed on October 24, 1929. Hoover attempted to provide assistance to those hardest hit by the economic disaster, but his belief that the private sector was best suited to provide relief, not the government, created the image that he was distancing himself when the country needed a strong leader.[8] By 1930, over four million people had lost their jobs. Across the country, shantytowns nicknamed "Hoovervilles" sprung up to house the homeless. The disconnect between Hoover and the suffering masses is perhaps best illustrated by the lavish, multicourse dinners he continued to enjoy in the White House dining room as bread lines formed in every city in America. He reportedly considered "economizing," but ultimately decided it would send the wrong message by conveying that he had lost confidence in the possibility of recovery.

The criticism and mounting pressure to solve the country's problems weighed heavily upon Hoover. As he navigated this unexpected and unprecedented crisis, his "medicine ball cabinet" became even more crucial in his struggle to lead during this difficult time. He reluctantly ran for a second term, knowing he had no real chance to win. Toward the end of 1932, Hoover said, "All the money in the world could not induce me to live over the last nine months. The conditions we have experienced make this office a compound hell."[9]

On March 3, 1933, his last day in office, his medicine ball cabinet presented him with this silver humidor engraved with a scene of the Hoover Ball court on the White House lawn, complete with images of his two dogs, to commemorate the time they had spent together. There were sixteen members of the "medicine ball cabinet," and each of their signatures appears on the humidor.

Ultimately, Hoover Ball accomplished its objective: Hoover lost those 25 pounds.

Franklin D. Roosevelt, 1933–1945: Fireside Chat Microphone

Franklin Delano Roosevelt won the 1932 presidential election by a landslide. Incumbent Herbert Hoover carried only five states—Pennsylvania, Connecticut, New Hampshire, Vermont, and Maine—winning just 59 electoral votes. No Republican in history had lost a presidential election as badly, except for the election of 1912 when Teddy Roosevelt's Bull Moose Party divided the votes. Roosevelt's sweeping victory had been made possible by "galvanizing immigrants, Catholics and Jews, farmers and industrial laborers, city dwellers and the rural poor into a vast coalition."[1]

From the moment he accepted the nomination of the Democratic Party, Roosevelt promised Americans a "New Deal" to combat the effects of an economic depression that had already gripped the nation for more than three years. The election was not just a battle between two political parties, but two fundamentally different approaches to recovery. Roosevelt believed in federal activism, which Hoover blasted as dangerous and expensive. In the end, 22,821,857 Americans supported Roosevelt's vision and voted for a change in direction.

Roosevelt inherited more problems than any president in recent memory. The unemployment rate hovered around 25 percent, and the nation's banking system was on the verge of collapse. Roosevelt knew he needed to speak directly to the American people, so he could both explain his plans for recovery and reassure them that the future would be brighter. By the 1930s, 90 percent of American households owned a radio, which made it the ideal way to reach the most people at once.

Franklin D. Roosevelt delivered his informal radio addresses called "Fireside Chats" into America's living rooms throughout his presidency.
FRANKLIN D. ROOSEVELT PRESIDENTIAL LIBRARY & MUSEUM

Radio shows for entertainment began in the 1910s, and KDKA, the first commercial radio station in the United States, started broadcasting from Wilkinsburg, Pennsylvania, in 1920.[2] According to the *Encyclopedia Britannica,* "broadcast radio astonished and delighted the public by providing news and entertainment with an immediacy never before thought possible."[3] Roosevelt wanted to harness that power to sell his far-reaching agenda of federal relief policies and programs. During his four terms as president, radio would become the first electronic mass medium, with enormous reach and influence.

Just eight days after his inauguration, on the evening of March 12, 1933, Americans turned on their radios and heard their new president say, "My friends, I want to talk for a few minutes with the people of the United States about banking." One of his first actions as president had been to declare a bank holiday, during which all banks in the country were ordered to close. A bank would only be allowed to reopen if a federal inspection deemed it to be solvent. In his first radio address, Roosevelt's tone was friendly and conversational, but firm. Hoover had attempted to communicate with the public via radio, but critics said he came across as stilted, impersonal, and condescending. In sharp contrast, Roosevelt sounded confident, yet pleasant, as he broke down a complicated idea into digestible chunks for his audience. He spoke clearly and slightly slower than his normal cadence.[4]

In that first broadcast, which would become known as a "fireside chat," Roosevelt explained a great deal of technical information about the country's financial system in colloquial fashion, including his plans to fix it:

I want to tell you what has been done in the last few days, why it was done, and what the next steps are going to be. I recognize that the many proclamations from State Capitols and from Washington, the legislation, the Treasury regulations, etc., couched for the most part in banking and legal terms should be explained for the benefit of the average citizen. I owe this in particular because of the fortitude and good temper with which everybody has accepted the inconvenience and hardships of the banking holiday. I know that when you understand what we in Washington have been about I shall continue to have your cooperation as fully as I have had your sympathy and help during the past week.

First of all let me state the simple fact that when you deposit money in a bank the bank does not put the money into a safe deposit vault. It invests your money in many different forms of credit—bonds, commercial paper, mortgages and many other kinds of loans. In other words, the bank puts your money to work to keep the wheels of industry and of agriculture turning around. A comparatively small part of the money you put into the bank is kept in currency—an amount which in normal times is wholly sufficient to cover the cash needs of the average citizen. In other words the total amount of all the currency in the country is only a small fraction of the total deposits in all of the banks.

What, then, happened during the last few days of February and the first few days of March? Because of undermined confidence on the part of the public, there was a general rush by a large portion of our population to turn bank deposits into currency or gold—a rush so great that the soundest banks could not get enough currency to meet the demand. The reason for this was that on the spur of the moment it was, of course, impossible to sell perfectly sound assets of a bank and convert them into cash except at panic prices far below their real value.

By the afternoon of March 3 scarcely a bank in the country was open to do business. Proclamations temporarily closing them in whole or in part had been issued by the Governors in almost all the states. It was then that I issued the proclamation providing for the nation-wide bank holiday, and this was the first step in the Government's reconstruction of our financial and economic fabric. . . .

It is possible that when the banks resume a very few people who have not recovered from their fear may again begin withdrawals. Let me make it clear that the banks will take care of all needs—and it is my belief that hoarding during the past week has become an exceedingly unfashionable pastime. It needs no prophet to tell you that when the people find that they can get their money— that they can get it when they want it for all legitimate purposes—the phantom of fear will soon be laid. People will again be glad to have their money where it will be safely taken care of and where they can use it conveniently at any time. I can assure you that it is safer to keep your money in a reopened bank than under the mattress.[5]

According to The History Channel, the bank holiday, combined with his informal radio address, achieved the desired effect. "When the banks opened again, the panicked 'bank runs' that people had feared did not materialize, showing that public confidence had been restored in some measure for the time being."[6] Feedback from the American public was overwhelmingly positive. One listener said, "Last evening as I listened to the President's broadcast I felt that he walked into my home, sat down and in plain and forceful language explained to me how he was tackling the job."[7]

Between March 1933 and June 1944, Roosevelt would give approximately 30 of his "fireside chats," a term coined by CBS reporter Harry Butcher on May 7, 1933. "The name stuck, as it perfectly evoked the comforting intent behind

Roosevelt's words, as well as their informal, conversational tone. Roosevelt took care to use the simplest possible language, concrete examples, and analogies in the fireside chats, so as to be clearly understood by the largest number of Americans. He began many of the nighttime chats with the greeting 'My friends,' and referred to himself as 'I' and the American people as 'you' as if addressing his listeners directly and personally."[8] Each broadcast ended with "The Star Spangled Banner," underscoring the patriotism and sense of duty that Roosevelt hoped to invoke with his speeches.

Although these "fireside chats" sounded informal, they were as carefully crafted as any other message Roosevelt delivered in other formats. It might have come across as "conversational," but the script itself had that tone built into it. According to the Library of Congress, a technical analysis of the "fireside chat" speeches reveals other factors that contributed to their success. "Most of the words were among the most commonly used in everyday English. And Roosevelt spoke more slowly than many other users of radio—120 to 130 words per minute while the political norm of the time approached 175–200 words. For clarity and emphasis of key points, he sometimes spoke as few as 100 words a minute. His vocal pacing was masterful for radio delivery."[9] His "fireside chats" almost always focused on a single issue, which Roosevelt would explain in familiar comparisons as if he were speaking to a neighbor over the backyard fence.

The "fireside chats" were among the highest-rated radio programs on the air, often reaching more people than the most popular entertainment shows of the era. According to the Hooper radio ratings service, nearly 54 million people (of roughly 82 million adult Americans) tuned in to the broadcast."[10] By the end of his presidency, it is estimated that two-thirds of the country had heard the president's voice, which was unprecedented at the time.[11]

Roosevelt was the first president to harness the power of communicating directly with his constituents, without the editorial filter from newspaper reporters and editors. In spite of the often unsettling news during the Depression and later World War II, the "reassuring nature" of his "fireside chats" would boost public confidence, as well as his approval rates, and "undoubtedly contributed to his unprecedented number of election wins."[12] Roosevelt carefully controlled his public image visually, believing that his physical disability from polio would be seen as weak. But through the power of radio, he could let his guard down and allow his voice to convey his strength as the nation's commander in chief.

Almost every president since Roosevelt has used radio, and later television, to speak directly to the American people. However, these addresses are mostly formal occasions, with the president either standing behind a podium or seated behind his desk in the Oval Office. Jimmy Carter evoked the feeling of a "fireside chat" on February 2, 1977, when he addressed the nation about the energy crisis, wearing a casual sweater and sitting in an easy chair near one of the White House fireplaces. In 1982, Ronald Regan began a series of 330 brief weekly radio talks, which marked the return of radio as a way for a president to reach the nation. But none of his successors would capture the imagination of the American people in the same way as Roosevelt did with his iconic "fireside chats," which helped a nation persevere through some of the darkest hours of the 20th century.

Harry S. Truman, 1945–1953: "The Buck Stops Here" Desk Sign

This iconic "The Buck Stops Here" sign sat on Harry S. Truman's desk in the Oval Office for most of his presidency. Truman often referred to it in public statements, including a speech at the National War College on December 19, 1952, when he said, "You know, it's easy for the Monday morning quarterback to say what the coach should have done, after the game is over. But when the decision is up before you—and on my desk I have a motto which says 'The Buck Stops Here'—the decision has to be made."[1]

According to *A Dictionary of Americanisms on Historical Principles*, the phrase "the buck stops here" comes from the expression "pass the buck" which means to pass the responsibility for something on to someone else. "The latter expression is said to have originated with the game of poker, in which a marker or counter, frequently in frontier days a knife with a buckhorn handle, was used to indicate the person whose turn it was to deal. If the player did not wish to deal he could pass the responsibility by passing the 'buck,' as the counter came to be called, to the next player."[2]

Truman understood that the president often had to make difficult decisions, and the ultimate responsibility for those decisions were his alone to bear. He would be tested fairly quickly after the death of Franklin D. Roosevelt. When he took office on April 12, 1945, the war in Europe was already winding down, but experts estimated that the war in Asia would continue for a year, and an invasion of Japan would bring heavy casualties. In August, Truman made the decision to use the atomic bomb, a top-secret weapon that had recently been tested. More than one hundred thousand Japanese citizens died instantly when bombs were dropped on Hiroshima and Nagasaki, with many more dying from radiation poisoning afterward. It brought an abrupt end to the fighting in the Pacific theater.[3]

Truman faced more difficult decisions while navigating a postwar world that was unlike anything that we had ever seen:

> In response to what it viewed as Soviet threats, the Truman administration constructed foreign policies to contain the Soviet Union's political power and counter its military strength. By 1949, Soviet and American policies had divided Europe into a Soviet-controlled bloc in the east and an American-supported grouping in the west. That same year, a communist government sympathetic to the Soviet Union came to power in China, the world's most populous nation. The Cold War between the United States and the Soviet Union, which would last for over forty years, had begun.[4]

The sign "The Buck Stops Here" that was on President Truman's desk in his White House office was made in the Federal Reformatory at El Reno, Oklahoma. Fred A. Canfil, then United States Marshal for the Western District of Missouri and a friend of Mr. Truman, saw a similar sign while visiting the Reformatory and asked the Warden if a sign like it could be made for President Truman. The sign was made and mailed to the President on October 2, 1945. It says "I'm from Missouri" on the other side.
HARRY S. TRUMAN PRESIDENTIAL LIBRARY, INDEPENDENCE, MISSOURI

After North Korea invaded its neighbor in the summer of 1950, Truman committed US troops to defend South Korea, which cost him politically as the stalemate dragged on. Domestically, Congress rejected many of his "Fair Deal" liberal policies. In 1952, Truman initially ran for reelection but ultimately withdrew from the Democratic Party nomination.

At the end of his presidency in January 1953, Truman again referred to the phrase in his farewell address, saying, "The President—whoever he is—has to decide. He can't pass the buck to anybody. No one else can do the deciding for him. That's his job."[5] The sign has been displayed at the Truman Presidential Library since 1957.

33

Dwight D. Eisenhower, 1953–1961: Globe

Dwight D. Eisenhower was a celebrated war hero who easily won the election of 1952. This globe was used in many photo ops at the White House, including when explorer Matt Henson, who was the first to reach the North Pole in 1909, met with Eisenhower in 1954.[1] In another famous photo, Eisenhower and Vice President Richard Nixon discussed Nixon's trip to the Far East in November 1953 while standing on either side of the globe. It was often seen in the background before and during his administration, symbolizing how he valued his global experiences in times of both war and peace.

Initially, Eisenhower had no interest in becoming president. He had rejected a clandestine offer from Harry S. Truman to run as his vice president in 1948, and in 1952 he was content to focus on his responsibilities as commander of NATO forces in Europe. Eventually Republican Party leaders convinced him to run, and he ended up winning 442 electoral votes.[2]

Cold War politics dominated much of his presidency. Although he kept the nation out of war, he did not achieve the lasting global peace that he had hoped for. In 1953 he debuted his national security policy "New Look," which focused on four key points:

- Maintaining the vitality of the US economy while still building sufficient strength to prosecute the Cold War
- Relying on nuclear weapons to deter Communist aggression or, if necessary, to fight a war

- Using the Central Intelligence Agency (CIA) to carry out secret or covert actions against governments or leaders "directly or indirectly responsive to Soviet control"
- Strengthening allies and winning the friendship of nonaligned governments[3]

Within six months of his inauguration, Eisenhower agreed to an armistice that ended the Korean conflict, which had become a liability for Truman. But in the end, he left his successor with a Cold War that was even more dangerous than when he took office.

Although he was popular with the public, he was often criticized by his contemporaries for delegating too much of his responsibilities to other White House workers. He was frequently seen fishing and golfing, and his "meandering, garbled answers to questions at press conferences" led some to question his understanding of important issues. However, his presidential papers, which were released in the 1970s, show evidence of a leader who was actively engaged in running the country behind the scenes.[4]

Dwight D. Eisenhower's globe illustrates how he valued his global experiences in both war and peace time. It was often seen in the background of presidential addresses and staged press photographs.
EISENHOWER PRESIDENTIAL LIBRARY, ABILENE, KANSAS

This globe, which was so important to Eisenhower, is on display in the recently renovated permanent exhibitions at the Eisenhower Presidential Library, Museum, and Boyhood Home. It is the first artifact the visitor encounters in the section "Waging Peace." Eisenhower's enduring legacy is that he was a leader who understood war, but valued peace more. "I hate war," he said in an address to the Canadian Club on January 10, 1946, "as only a soldier who has lived it can, only as one who has seen its brutality, its futility, its stupidity."[5]

John F. Kennedy, 1961–1963: PT 109 Coconut Husk Paperweight

Although this coconut husk predates John F. Kennedy's presidency, the staff at the John F. Kennedy Presidential Library and Museum believe it "represents a turning point in his life, one that would shape him as a man and president. Its importance to him is reflected in the fact that the husk, by then sealed in plastic, remained a prominent feature on his desk in the Oval Office."[1]

Kennedy joined the US Navy in 1941 and was stationed in the Solomon Islands in the Pacific Ocean during the early years of World War II. On August 3, 1943, Lieutenant Kennedy was in command of Patrol Torpedo Craft (PT) 109 when it was struck by the Japanese destroyer *Amagiri*. The crew was thrown into the water. With the Japanese occupying all of the islands nearby, the crew decided to swim three and a half miles to an island called Plum Pudding, which was also known as Bird Island.

Kennedy was a strong swimmer who had been on the swim team at Harvard, but only a few of his crew were also good swimmers. Two could not swim at all. Kennedy swam with injured engineer Patrick McMahon's lifejacket belt in his teeth, and the other seven men took turns pulling or pushing a plank with two of the men who could not swim at all.[2]

When he finally reached the island, Kennedy collapsed on the beach from exhaustion. When a Japanese barge passed close to shore, he made the decision to swim into a passage where American PT boats routinely operated. After treading water for nearly an hour without seeing any American boats, he decided to swim back. Strong currents on the return trip nearly killed him.

John F. Kennedy wrote a message on this coconut husk after his PT boat was destroyed by the Japanese in the Pacific Ocean during World War II. His father had it made into a paperweight, which Kennedy kept on his desk in the Oval Office.

He stopped on Leorava Island, southeast of Bird Island, to rest before the last leg of the trip. Once back on Bird Island, Kennedy slept through the day. He made Ross promise to make the same trip that night, but he did not see any American boats either.[3]

Kennedy and Ross continued to island hop, eventually finding a Japanese shipwreck with some candy and a tin of fresh water. They also found two islanders, Biuku Gasa and Eroni Kumana, who had been working as scouts for the Allies. They showed Kennedy how to carve a message on a husk of green coconut. They set out in their canoe with the message, which read:

NAURO ISL
COMMANDER . . . NATIVE KNOWS
POS'IT . . . HE CAN PILOT . . . 11 ALIVE
NEED SMALL BOAT . . . KENNEDY[4]

On August 8, six days after they were shipwrecked, the men were finally rescued.

Kennedy once said that World War II shaped his entire generation. "It was and is our single greatest moment. . . . It serves as a breakwall between the indolence of our youths and the earnestness of our manhoods," he said. His experience commanding PT 109 would be used during his political career "as evidence that Kennedy was the embodiment of a modern hero, someone with proven ability to lead despite his youth. His status as a veteran also gave him a powerful shared experience with close to half of Americans of voting age in 1960."[5]

The US Navy kept the coconut husk and returned it to Kennedy. According to Janice Hodson of the John F. Kennedy Presidential Library and Museum, "In July 1944 Joseph P. Kennedy had the husk encased in plastic as a memento for his son, a process carried out under the oversight of Dr. George Sperti at the Institutum Divi Thomae in Cincinnati, Ohio. To make the rescue message more legible, the incised letters were embedded with carbon before the fragment was encased."[6] The paperweight on his desk would be a constant reminder of Kennedy's leadership and bravery, and it is a treasured artifact in his presidential library's collection.

Lyndon B. Johnson, 1963–1969: Desk Blotter

When Lyndon B. Johnson suddenly became president after John F. Kennedy's assassination, he vowed to keep working on the issues that had been important to his predecessor. He called his sweeping progressive agenda "The Great Society," which tackled such issues as civil rights, poverty, education, and the environment. This silver desk blotter, a gift from his Cabinet members before he left office, is titled "Landmark Laws of the Lyndon B. Johnson Administration," and it outlines his many successes as president. Although he won by a landslide in the election of 1964, he chose not to seek a second term, largely because of his declining popularity due to his handling of the Vietnam War.

Johnson's mandate in 1964 allowed him to pursue a wide variety of legislation that would improve the lives of countless Americans. The subtitle of the blotter reads "With these acts President Lyndon B. Johnson and the Congress wrote a record of hope and opportunity for America." Together, they waged a "War on Poverty" that sought to address issues of inequality. Successful programs that still exist today include Head Start, which provides early education opportunities for disadvantaged families and the Legal Services Corporation, which promotes equal access to justice through local legal aid programs. The work Johnson led did have an impact:

> Between 1965 and 1968, expenditures targeted at the poor doubled, from $6 billion to $12 billion, and then doubled again to $24.5 billion by 1974. The billions of dollars spent to aid the poor did have effective results, especially in job

training and job placement programs. Partly as a result of these initiatives—and also due to a booming economy—the rate of poverty in America declined significantly during the Johnson years.[1]

Kennedy had been committed to passing a civil rights act to end segregation in the South, and Johnson vowed to continue working toward its passage. Johnson was from the South, allowing him to forge a bipartisan effort to support the Civil Rights Act of 1964, which banned segregation in all "public accommodations involved in interstate commerce."[2]

In 1965, civil rights activists turned to voting rights. Since the end of Reconstruction, local governments in the South had created barriers to voting for African Americans. In addition to flat-out intimidation, local voting restrictions included literacy tests, "good character" tests, and poll taxes. After Black demonstrators were attacked by police dogs on national television in Selma, Alabama, Johnson seized the opportunity created by public outrage to gain support for the Voting Rights Act of 1965. The act banned literacy tests and set up federal marshals and registrars to register Black voters. Accord-

Lyndon B. Johnson's administration passed an astonishing array of legislation, which were commemorated in this desk blotter presented to him by his Cabinet.
LYNDON B. JOHNSON PRESIDENTIAL LIBRARY

ing to the Miller Center, "The results were immediate and significant. Black voter turnout tripled within four years, coming very close to white turnouts throughout the South."[3]

During the Johnson years, other legislation established the National Endowment for the Humanities and the National Endowment for the Arts, provided consumer protections, and established environmental regulations that addressed pollution in the nation's air and water. The blotter list includes the following acts: Indian Vocational Training, Kennedy Cultural Center, Pesticide Controls, Federal Highway, Food Stamps, Federal Employee Health Benefits, Medicare, Fair Immigration Law, Mental Health Facilities, Child Health, GI Life Insurance, Military Pay Increase, Child Nutrition, Traffic Safety, Bail Reform, Minimum Wage Increase, Scientific Knowledge Exchange, Freedom of Information, Flammable Fabrics, Public Broadcasting, Summer Youth Programs, Fair Housing, Aircraft Noise Abatement, Gas Pipeline Safety, Guaranteed Student Loans, and Gun Controls.

In spite of his many successes in reforming domestic policies, Johnson's legacy remains controversial. "Many of his initiatives for the arts, for the environment, for poverty, for racial justice, and for workplace safety angered many economic and social conservatives and became the targets of alienated white voters and tax revolters. The reaction to his Great Society and to broader trends helped spawn a dramatic political polarization in the United States that some historians have labeled a conservative counterrevolution."[4] Johnson left the presidency with a very low approval rating and spent a "restless" four years in retirement before passing away at his beloved Texas ranch.[5]

36

Richard Nixon, 1969–1974: Easy Chair

Richard Nixon's legacy has been tainted by the Watergate break-in and the infamous "tapes" he often secretly recorded of White House conversations, obscuring his quick rise in politics from congressman to senator to vice president between 1946 and 1952. His political aspirations were interrupted by John F. Kennedy's narrow victory in the election of 1960, but he finally won the White House in 1968.

Nixon was an intellectual, but he was also socially awkward and often ill at ease at the very ceremonies featuring the pomp and circumstance he adored.[1] "He was an intellectual appealing to a public that puts low value on eggheads," wrote Tom Wicker in his chapter on Nixon in the essay collection *Character Above All*. "I don't mean an intellectual in the stereotypical sense of a cloistered scholar; I mean that Nixon was a highly intelligent man who relied greatly on his own intelligence and that of others, who had a considerable capacity to read and understand technical papers, who retreated to a room alone and wrote in longhand on a yellow legal pad the gist of his major speeches, who impressed associates with his ability to evaluate disinterestedly the pros and cons of a problem."[2]

A symbol of his intellect is his humble easy chair, which served as the backdrop for Nixon's research, speech writing, and decision-making as president. According to Christine Mickey, acting supervisory museum curator of the Richard Nixon Presidential Library and Museum, "This chair was purchased by Pat Nixon as a gift and used by President Nixon in the Lincoln Sitting Room, where he regularly immersed himself in isolation and did his most

This humble easy chair, which Richard Nixon used in the Lincoln Sitting Room at the White House, has come to symbolize Richard Nixon's intellect.

important thinking and writing. The image of this object reflects not only on the policy accomplishments of his presidency but the intellectual intensity of his entire public life."[3]

There are many examples of important work done while sitting in this chair. In his diary entries, H. R. Haldeman, Nixon's administrative assistant and chief of staff, specifically mentions the easy chair three times, in reference to reviewing a speech, negotiating peace in Vietnam, and choosing a suitable backdrop for a televised address:

January 20, 1970

At midday he called [Henry] Kissinger, [John] Ehrlichman and me over to EOB. Was lounging in his easy chair with the speech. Said he wanted to read it to us. First, a long discussion regarding HEW veto. Made point he doesn't really care if they do override—because that puts the spending burden on Congress. Changed timing plan—will veto Monday night.[4]

October 12, 1972

Henry [Kissinger] and [Alexander] Haig got back from Paris and had dinner with the President at 7:00. I went home from the airport, got a call at home saying the President wanted me at the dinner, so I drove back in to the White House. We met at 6:45 in the EOB office [Charles "Chuck"] Colson there at the time and the President went over some odds and ends with Chuck on reaction to today, then Kissinger and Haig arrived, and Chuck left. We sat in the inner office, and as soon as Chuck went out the door, Kissinger opened by saying, well, you've got three for three, Mr. President. The President was sitting over in his easy chair; Kissinger, Haig and I were sitting at the table. The President was a little incredulous at first, and sort of queried Henry a bit. Henry started to outline the agreement from the, his secret red folder, made the point overall that we got a much better deal by far than we had expected. There are still five items to negotiate but, Kissinger's convinced that he can do this. The net effect is that it leaves Thieu in office. We get a stand-in-place cease-fire on October 30 or 31. They permit the South Vietnamese to hold the prisoners in jail. They have to agree to work together to set up a Council of International, or National Concord and Reconciliation, but any action by this council has to be by unanimous vote, so it can't effectively hurt Thieu any. The cease-fire would be followed by a complete withdrawal of troops within 60 days and a return of the POW's in 60 days, so we'd have everything done by the end of the year. He then said that

North Vietnam, one of the agreements is that we'd provide an economic aid program for five years.[5]

November 1, 1972

The President spent a lot of time today with Ray Price, working over the various speeches they've developed—a good one on health that he's going to do on Friday, and then foreign policy on Saturday for the Sunday papers, and ten goals Sunday for the Monday papers—all radio speeches—and he's polished up the TV speech. He's concerned about delivery on the TV thing and decided not to use the easy chair, but would rather will sit behind a desk and do it as a desk setting but in the library with the books back of him, so that it looks like a library. He also wants to get the maximum TV coverage that we can out of it, and he agreed late this afternoon to tape it rather than doing it live—if we would agree to do it as a sudden death tape with no replays, just leaving the flubs in and so on. We reviewed the general situation in our poll standing, etcetera, and he seems to feel now that we're in good shape.[6]

This easy chair, which was a witness to so many important conversations in Nixon's presidency, is part of his presidential library's collection today. A life-sized statue of Nixon sitting in the chair, pen in hand and making notes on a legal pad, is displayed in the corner of a dark gallery cast in blue light. On the walls are "passages from his legendary yellow legal pad notes that he often penned in the intimate space."[7]

37

Gerald Ford, 1974–1977: Statuette of Elephant and Donkey

Gerald Ford's path to the White House was anything but conventional. He was the first person nominated vice president under the Twenty-fifth Amendment after Spiro Agnew resigned on October 10, 1973, and pleaded no contest to federal charges of income tax evasion. Less than a year later, in the aftermath of the Watergate scandal, Richard Nixon resigned on August 8, 1974. In his swearing-in speech, Ford said, "I assume the Presidency under extraordinary circumstances. . . . This is an hour of history that troubles our minds and hurts our hearts."[1]

Prior to his peculiar climb to the White House, Ford had spent 25 years as a congressman from Michigan. His "warm personality, his knowledge of the budget and appropriations process, and his willingness to accommodate his opponents propelled his rise to the Republican leadership."[2] The bipartisanship that was so important to Ford is exemplified in the statuette he kept on his congressional desk. According to Donald Holloway, former curator of the Gerald R. Ford Presidential Museum, "It is a bronze piece depicting a donkey and an elephant, each sitting on the ground with their backs to one another. It was to Ford a symbol of bipartisanship, a theme he played on often in his presidency. He appealed to it in his swearing-in speech and in other speeches he made before Congress. He often said he had no enemies, only adversaries. A Democrat, Daniel Patrick Moynihan, served as his ambassador to the United Nations. He sought to work closely with both Carl Albert and Tip O'Neill. Such bipartisanship was a critical component, Ford believed, in his efforts to bind the wounds suffered because of the Vietnam War and Watergate."[3]

Ford took office with incredible support from the media, the public, and politicians from both sides, but it would be short-lived support: "His decision—after only one month in office—to pardon former president Nixon ended this honeymoon."[4] A sluggish economy and constant battles with Congress over his policy priorities weakened him politically. When he faced Jimmy Carter, who called himself a "Washington outsider," in the election of 1976, he had little chance of winning.

Ford's brief time in the White House was largely undistinguished. "His record during that time was decidedly mixed; his domestic and foreign policies were neither spectacular successes nor disastrous failures. He faced considerable political opposition from Democrats in Congress and from conservative Republicans. But scholars largely agree on Ford's greatest contribution: as president, Ford's decency and honesty did much to restore the American public's faith in its political leaders."[5]

This statuette of an elephant and donkey symbolized bipartisanship to Gerald Ford.
GERALD R. FORD PRESIDENTIAL MUSEUM

Jimmy Carter, 1977–1981: Hungarian Crown

Jimmy Carter's election against Gerald Ford, the first unelected president in US history whose popularity was in decline from the beginning, was closer than it should have been. Both candidates made gaffes in the days leading up to the election, which Carter won by a narrow margin. Like Ford, Carter would struggle as president. As the Miller Center succinctly describes it, "Jimmy Carter's one-term presidency is remembered for the events that overwhelmed it—inflation, energy crisis, war in Afghanistan, and hostages in Iran."[1]

Carter's image was austere, casual, and honest. Even his inauguration festivities were low-key. He often wore a cardigan sweater when he gave presidential addresses, and he was known for his strong moral compass. According to Brittany Parris, supervisory archivist at the Jimmy Carter Presidential Library and Museum, returning the Holy Crown of Hungary in 1978 has often been characterized as an example of Carter's commitment to "doing the right thing," even when it might not be "politically expedient."[2]

The United States took possession of this important piece of Hungarian history near the end of World War II. With the Soviet army approaching, the Hungarian Crown guard gave it to US Army officers for safekeeping, and it was ultimately put into storage at Fort Knox.[3] In 1977, Carter decided it was finally time to return the crown to Hungary. According to a memo from Hamilton Jordan, Carter's chief of staff, Hungarian Americans were generally against returning the crown.

Former government officials and educated Hungarians may have a more enlightened view of this matter, but the average Hungarian American is opposed
to this action because the alleged benefit to the people of Hungary has not been
explained and is difficult to explain. Their reaction to our return of the Crown
is emotional and not an enlightened view. . . . We mislead ourselves to think that
the Hungarian-American community is closely divided on this issue. It is not. If
it were, you would not have had members of Congress and the leaders of all of
the Captive Nation organizations protesting this decision. It is one thing for us
to suffer domestically with a group of people in pursuit of a major policy that
is important to us and the world (the Mideast, for example). It is quite another
for us to suffer politically for an action that has very little—if any—redeeming
features. We are alienating the Hungarian community in this country in hopes
of gaining some intangible benefit from the Communist regime in Hungary.
The political trade-offs do not seem acceptable to me.[4]

Árpád Göncz, president of the Republic of Hungary, presented Jimmy Carter with this
exact replica of the Holy Crown of Hungary on March 18, 1998.
JIMMY CARTER PRESIDENTIAL LIBRARY

In a letter to the president dated November 7, 1977, Jeane Dixon wrote, "For more than thirty years, we have insisted that we would never turn it over to their Soviet-backed rulers. American Presidents of both parties have reaffirmed their sacred trust. It must not be betrayed now. Your intentions in this matter have been noble: to show the world that the United States has no selfish interest in the Crown and to make of it an instrument of good will among nations. But there is an even better way to accomplish those purposes." She proposed bringing the crown out of storage and displaying it in the United States, under a triple guard: "Let one guard be an American, because our country was entrusted with the Crown. Let one be a member of the Pope's Swiss Guards from the Vatican, because the Crown originally came from the Papacy to King Stephen one thousand years ago. And let one guard be a volunteer from among the brave Hungarian freedom fighters who fled their country after Soviet tanks crushed their revolt in 1956."[5]

In spite of strong opposition from the public and within his own staff, the Carter administration held a ceremony to return the crown on January 6, 1978, at the Hungarian Parliament. Carter was playing a political long game which proved to be beneficial. "The return of the Crown led to a marked improvement in US-Hungarian relations and was a major factor contributing to the historic changes in Hungary following the fall of communism in Eastern Europe."[6]

On March 18, 1998, Árpád Göncz, president of the Republic of Hungary, presented Carter with an exact replica of the crown at the Jimmy Carter Presidential Library and Museum. During the ceremony, Carter said, "This replica of the Crown of Hungary is a wonderful gift, and I am proud to accept it on behalf of the people of the United States. The people of Hungary trusted us to keep one of their greatest treasures. We returned it when conditions permitted. This replica of the magnificent Crown is a generous and gracious gesture of the abiding faith and trust that exists between our two countries."[7] The replica was placed on permanent view in the museum.

Just as Jordan had feared, returning the crown did little to improve Carter's image. Media coverage throughout his presidency was generally unfavorable. He made things worse with the so-called malaise speech, in which he lamented "a lack of confidence in America's purpose and its future" that he blamed on the American people themselves.[8] Ultimately America would choose Ronald Reagan in the election of 1980, whose fresh optimism felt a lot better than Carter's continuous gloom and doom. Polling showed Carter far behind, which proved true on Election Day. Reagan won, capturing 440 electoral votes.

Ronald Reagan, 1981–1989: Piece of the Berlin Wall

One of the most famous quotes from Ronald Regan's presidency comes from his speech on June 12, 1987, in West Berlin when he said, "Mr. Gorbachev, tear down this wall!" He was standing in front of the Brandenburg Gate, an 18th-century monument that had been incorporated into the Berlin Wall, which divided East Germany from West Germany. A piece of the wall is now part of the Ronald Reagan Presidential Library and Museum's collection. It is situated on the south lawn of the museum, in a place of honor not far from Reagan's grave.

The Berlin Wall was built in 1961 by the East German government during the escalating Cold War. After World War II, Germany's capitol was divided into four sections. The Allies controlled the western part, and the Soviets controlled the eastern part. The western sections of the country came together in May 1949 to form the Federal Republic of Germany (West Germany). The Soviet Union created the German Democratic Republic (East Germany) in October 1949. The border between the two countries closed in 1952, and East German citizens were restricted from leaving the country.[1] The wall followed the entire border of West Berlin, which was already an island inside East Germany.

Over the years, the Berlin Wall had become a powerful symbol of the divide between Communist countries and the free world. In 1987, Berlin was celebrating its 750th anniversary, and other world leaders had scheduled visits. Reagan was planning a tour of Europe but did not originally intend to

This section of the Berlin Wall was moved to the Reagan Presidential Library in April 1990. On the western side, it is decorated with a colorful butterfly and flowers, but the eastern side is blank.
RONALD REAGAN PRESIDENTIAL LIBRARY

visit West Berlin. He changed his plans, and speechwriter Peter Robinson got started on his remarks.

On an advance trip to gather material, Robinson attended a dinner party with a small group of West Berlin residents. He had been told by an American diplomat that Reagan should avoid grandstanding and any inflammatory statements about the Berlin Wall, because the citizens had "long ago gotten used to the structure that encircled them." His dining companions disagreed. The hostess became visibly upset. "A gracious woman, she had suddenly grown angry," said Robinson. "Her face was red. She made a fist with one hand and pounded it into the palm of the other. 'If this man Gorbachev is serious with his talk of glasnost and perestroika,' she said, 'he can prove it. He can get rid of this wall.'"[2] Robinson had found his inspiration.

The State Department and the National Security Council objected to the draft, but Reagan himself insisted that the famous line be left as written. In the limousine ride on the day of the speech, Reagan smiled and said, "The boys at State are going to kill me, but it's the right thing to do."[3] The context of the speech called for arms reduction, but the section that everyone remembers was this:

> Behind me stands a wall that encircles the free sectors of this city, part of a vast system of barriers that divides the entire continent of Europe. . . . Standing before the Brandenburg Gate, every man is a German, separated from his fellow men. Every man is a Berliner, forced to look upon a scar. . . . As long as this gate is closed, as long as this scar of a wall is permitted to stand, it is not the German question alone that remains open, but the question of freedom for all mankind. . . .
>
> General Secretary Gorbachev, if you seek peace, if you seek prosperity for the Soviet Union and Eastern Europe, if you seek liberalization, come here to this gate.
>
> Mr. Gorbachev, open this gate!
>
> Mr. Gorbachev, tear down this wall![4]

On November 9, 1989, a few days after thousands of East Germans demonstrated for democracy, the East German state council announced plans to open the gates. Overwhelmed by the massive crowds who came to the wall, border security went ahead and let anyone cross through to West Berlin. That night, people began dismantling the wall with sledgehammers and pickaxes.

Most of the wall was destroyed, but some sections were preserved as a memorial. This section was moved to the Reagan Presidential Library in April 1990. On the western side, it is decorated with a colorful butterfly and flowers, but the eastern side is blank. At its dedication, Ronald Reagan said, "Let our children and grandchildren come here and see this wall and reflect on what it meant to history. Let them understand that only vigilance and strength will deter tyranny."[5]

George H. W. Bush, 1989–1993: Letter to Family

To best illustrate George H. W. Bush's presidency, the staff at the George H. W. Bush Presidential Library and Museum chose this New Year's Eve letter to his family, typed by Bush himself with handwritten corrections just days before the Persian Gulf War began.[1] His words demonstrate the careful consideration of a commander in chief who is about to make the difficult decision to launch a major offensive military operation.

According to Jay Patton, Supervisory Curator at the George H. W. Bush Presidential Library and Museum, the letter reveals a great deal about Bush's character:

> In his letter, President Bush discusses the decision to proceed with Operation DESERT STORM in the coming month. This letter, more than any other holding, captures who President Bush was as a leader. It demonstrates his strong commitment to family, as well as the difficult decisions a president often encounters. It highlights his respect for the Office of the President of the United States and the awesome power it carries. The letter is unique among our holdings in that it covers so many areas of President Bush's administration: foreign policy, diplomacy, military affairs, political dealings, the checks and balances of our government, the importance of family, and respect for human lives. It shows a very personal side of President Bush, and it is a great illustration of who he was and how he approached the presidency.[2]

Dear George, Jeb, Neil, Marvin, Doro.

I am writing this letter on the last day of 1991./

First, I can't begin to tell you how great it was to have you here
at Camp David. I loved the games (the Marines are still smarting
over their 1 and 2 record), I loved Christmas Day, marred only by the absence
of Sam and Ellie. I loved the movies- some of 'em- I loved
the laughs. Most of all, I loved seeing you together. We are a family blessed; and
Christmas simply reinforced all that.

I hope I didn't seem moody. I tried not to.

When I came into this job I vowed that I would never ring my hands
and talk about "the loneliest job in the world"
or ring my hands about the "pressures or the trials".

Having said that I have been concerned about what lies ahead.
There is no 'loneliness' though because I am backed by a first rate
team of knowledgeable and committed people. No President has been more
blessed in this regard..

I have thought long and hard about what might have to be done.
As I write this letter at Year's end, there is still some hope
that Iraq's dictator will pull out of Kuwait. I vary on this . Sometimes
I think he might, at others I think he simply is too unrealistic- too
ignorant of what he might face. I have the peace of mind that comes from knowing
that we have tried hard for peace. We have gone to the uN ;we have formed an historic
coalition; there have been diplomatic initiatives from country after country.
And so, here we are a scant 16 days from a very important

date- the date set by the uN for his total compliance with all UN resolutions

including getting out of Kuwait- totally.

I guess what I want you to know as a father is this:

Every Human life is precious. When the question is asked "How many lives

are you willing to sacrifice"- it tears at my heart. The answer ,of course, is

none- none at all. We have waited to give sanctions a chance, we have moved

a tremendous force so as to reduce the risk to every American soldier

if force has to be used, but the question of loss of life still lingers and plagues the heart. .

My mind goes back to history:

How many lives might have been saved if appeasement had given way to force

earlier on in the late '30's or earliest '40's? How many Jews might have been

sapred the gas chambers, or how many Polish patriots might be alive today?

I look at todays crisis as "good vs. "evil".... yes, it is that clear.

I know my stance must cause you a little grief from time to time and this

hurts me; but here at 'years end I just wanted you to know that I feel:

        - every human life is precious.. the little Iraqi kids' too.

        - Principle must be adhered to- Saddam cannot profit in any

way at all from his aggression and from his brutalizing the people of Kuwait.

        - and sometimes in life you have to act as you think best-you

can't compromise, you can't give in,...even if your critics are loud and numerous,

In his New Year's Eve letter to his family, George H. W. Bush discusses the decision to proceed with Operation DESERT STORM in the coming days.

The Persian Gulf War arose from unfinished peace negotiations after an August 1988 cease-fire brokered by the United Nations to end the Iran-Iraq War. In July 1990, it appeared that the two nations would be able to come to a peace agreement. Feeling empowered by widespread support of Arab countries against Iran, two weeks later Saddam Hussein accused Kuwait of siphoning oil from oil fields along its border with Iraq. On August 2, 1990, Hussein sent troops into Kuwait and formally annexed the country as Iraq's "19th province" six days later. World leaders condemned his actions, and the US Air Force began sending fighter planes to Saudi Arabia as part of Operation Desert Shield.[3]

The United Nations Security Council set a deadline of January 15, 1991, for Iraq to withdraw troops from Kuwait. If Iraq did not comply, the coalition forces would use "all necessary means of force" against them. This crucial period is when Bush was writing his letter to his family. The most poignant passage describes the value of human life:

> I guess what I want you to know as a father is this: Every human life is precious. When the question is asked "How many lives are you willing to sacrifice"—it tears at my heart. The answer, of course, is none—none at all. We have waited to give sanctions a chance, we have moved a tremendous force so as to reduce the risk to every American soldier if force has to be used, but the question of loss of life still lingers and plagues the heart.

Iraq did not withdraw from Kuwait. Operation DESERT STORM began on January 17, with massive US airstrikes over Iraq, targeting communications, oil refineries, and weapons facilities. The objective was to gain as much ground as possible in the air, to minimize combat on the ground. The war became known as the "Video Game War" for the nightly news broadcast coverage of sophisticated military equipment, including cruise missiles, stealth bombers, "smart" bombs equipped with laser guidance systems, and infrared night-bombing technology.[4]

On February 24, the ground offensive Operation DESERT SABRE began. Bush declared a cease-fire on February 28, and Iraq agreed to recognize Kuwait's sovereignty and remove all of its weapons of mass destruction. Although the war was initially viewed as a decisive victory for the coalition forces, it contributed to political unrest in the region that would lead to increased terrorist attacks in the coming years.

41

Bill Clinton, 1993–2001: Saxophone

When he was elected in 1992, Bill Clinton became one of the youngest men to ever serve as president. During the campaign, he used his image as a member of the younger, hipper baby boom generation to appeal to a broader range of voters, including young first-time voters. His appearance on the Arsenio Hall Show on June 3, 1992, was designed to maximize his *je ne sais quoi* and set him apart from his opponents, incumbent George H. W. Bush and third-party candidate Ross Perot.

Clinton loved music from an early age. According to the Metropolitan Museum of Art, "He practiced every day, sometimes as many as four hours at a time. He loved jazz, played in his school's jazz ensemble, and won first chair in Arkansas's All-State Band. As a teenager, he even entertained the idea of pursuing music as a career."[1] He pursued a career in politics, but his music remained a treasured hobby.

Clinton's appearance on a late-night talk show was unprecedented. Presidential hopefuls typically limited their media appearances to serious news shows only. Media adviser Mandy Grunwald began planning a cost-effective alternative to traditional campaigning that would give Clinton the boost he needed. "The convention wasn't until July, so we had five or six weeks and very little money," she said. "We realized that people needed to know more about Bill Clinton. So I had written a memo saying we ought to do these kinds of softer talk shows. In terms of picking [which one], Arsenio Hall was serious with guests and oftentimes talked a little policy."[2]

Arsenio's sense of style completely redesigned Clinton's appearance, according to senior strategist Paul Begala. "When we got there, Arsenio looked at Clinton's very boring striped tie and said, 'Man, you cannot wear that on my show.' Arsenio disappeared, came back, and gave Clinton some loud yellow tie. I reached into my pocket and pulled out my Ray-Ban Wayfarers and said, 'Governor, you've got to wear my glasses.' He looked at [senior strategist

Bill Clinton broke with tradition when he appeared on *The Arsenio Hall Show* and played the saxophone during his presidential campaign in 1992. Czech Republic President Havel presented this saxophone to Clinton during his trip to Europe in January 1994.

WILLIAM J. CLINTON PRESIDENTIAL LIBRARY

James] Carville who said, 'Governor, anything pre-Beatles, I decide. Anything post-Beatles, Paul decides. This is a post-Beatles call.' When Clinton quit laughing, he said, 'All right. We'll wear the glasses.' Those glasses, they became famous. I donated them to the Clinton library."[3]

Michael Wolff, the show's musical director, listened to him play at practice. "You could tell he'd been a good high school saxophonist," Wolff said. "He wasn't great, but he was good. We spent time together and then afterward our whole band said, 'Look, man, if you win, we'd like to play the inauguration.' He was true to his word and we went and played the Kennedy Center on his first inauguration."[4]

Clinton talked to Arsenio, who asked him serious questions that voters would want to know. Then he played a sax solo with the show's band, performing "Heartbreak Hotel" and "God Bless the Child." His appearance was a hit with mainstream America but was deeply criticized by mainstream media. Begala recalled that the traditional news shows were "appalled and aghast," which only showed them that they were on the right track to win the election. He went on to appear on *Larry King Live* and MTV, with saxophone in hand. The appearances reinvigorated his campaign and ultimately helped him with the election.

There are several saxophones associated with Clinton. This one, from the collection of the Clinton Presidential Library and Museum, was presented to President Clinton during his trip to Europe in January 1994. It is made of brass with mother-of-pearl keys and is engraved with the signature of President Havel of the Czech Republic. Clinton donated the saxophone he played at his inauguration to the American Jazz Museum in Kansas City, Missouri in 2007.[5]

The National Music Museum's collection contains the "Number One Bill Clinton" limited-edition tenor saxophone. Inspired by Clinton's appearance on *The Arsenio Hall Show*, Peter J. La Placa, president and CEO of the L.A. Sax Company, began production of the LA-42T Presidential Model saxophone in 1993. The unique patriotic design is striking: "The saxophone features lacquer on the brass keys and the interior of the instrument's bell. The exterior touts a baked-epoxy finish in metallic fire red, diamond metallic white, and reflex blue, artistically blended with a field of brilliant white stars throughout the bell flare. Touches are accented with mother-of-pearl inlays." After it was presented to him in the Oval Office, Clinton played a few tunes on it, and then turned it over to the National Music Museum for their collection, saying, "That is the most beautiful saxophone I have ever seen."[6]

George W. Bush, 2001–2009: Bullhorn

Less than a year after his controversial presidential election, George W. Bush would lead the nation through the aftermath of arguably the most horrific tragedy in American history. On September 11, 2001, at 8:46 a.m., hijacked American Airlines Flight 11 crashed into the North Tower of the World Trade Center. At 9:03 a.m., hijacked United Airlines Flight 175 crashed into the South Tower. Two minutes later, in a second-grade classroom at Emma E. Booker Elementary School in Sarasota, Florida, White House chief of staff Andrew Card whispers into Bush's ear, "A second plane has hit the second tower. America is under attack."[1] The look on his face is a mixture of shock and a herculean effort to stay calm in front of the children.

Veteran ABC News journalist Ann Compton, who was in the press pool assigned to travel with the president, was sitting in the back of the classroom that day. What she saw was already extraordinary. "No one interrupts a president, not even in front of second graders," she said.[2] Bush hurried into the school cafeteria, where the news agencies had already set up their live cameras for a planned speech about education. He kept his remarks very brief, speaking for just over one minute. "Terrorism against our nation will not stand," he said. "And now if you would join me in a moment of silence."[3]

Meanwhile, the Secret Service was scrambling to get the president back on board Air Force One. Bush would enter from the front of the aircraft, and the reporters were funneled to the rear stairs. The bomb squad rushed to check all of their bags, in case any weapons had been planted in them. The usual quick flight back to Washington, D.C., would take nine and a half hours as Bush was kept in the air for his safety, accompanied by F-16 fighter jets.

In spite of all the capabilities of the modern Air Force One aircraft, its limitations were exposed that day:

> Those first hours were a nightmare that sharpened the frustration for the president. Air Force One is a flying White House. It has awesome features: secure phone lines, a hospital cabin, wiring shielded against attack, televisions embedded into the bulkhead walls throughout the aircraft. This was, however, before the age of digital communications and satellite TV. The president was flying blind. He was only able to watch hazy images on the TV screens because the signal was so faint from local TV stations below. Adding to his frustration were the high-altitude weakness of his secure phone lines and the jammed circuits on the ground.[4]

George Bush spoke to 9/11 first responders at Ground Zero using this bullhorn on September 14, 2001.
GEORGE W. BUSH PRESIDENTIAL LIBRARY AND MUSEUM

The plane did not have enough fuel to continue circling in the air, and in-flight refueling is considered too dangerous with the president onboard, so the plane landed at Barksdale Air Force Base in Shreveport, Louisiana. Bush wanted to make another statement to the public to reassure everyone that the United States government was still functioning. At 12:36 p.m., his speech began, "Freedom itself was attacked this morning by a faceless coward and freedom will be defended," he said. "I want to reassure the American people that the full resources of the Federal Government are working to assist local authorities to save lives and to help the victims of these attacks. Make no mistake: The United States will hunt down and punish those responsible for these cowardly acts."[5] One hour later, the plane took off again, with only a handful of reporters on board, destination undisclosed.

Although the reporters were not informed, Air Force One planned to land at Offutt Air Force Base in Omaha, Nebraska, the location of Strategic Command (STRATCOM). "Because STRATCOM has to be able to communicate securely with people worldwide in a moment's notice as part of its nuclear mission, it has among the best communications systems in the world," according to *News Now Omaha*.[6] Bush was able to video chat with his national security team at Offutt, which was also chosen because it is more secure than the average base.

For Bush, connecting with the American public was paramount. Years later, in a History Channel documentary, he said, "I knew I needed to give an address to the nation that night, and I damn sure wasn't gonna give it from a bunker in Omaha, Nebraska."[7] Over the objections of his advisors, Bush insisted on returning to the White House. Air Force One landed at Andrews Air Force Base around 7:00 p.m., where Marine One was waiting to take him home.

In the days that followed, Bush wanted to be as visible as possible, to reassure the nation that he understood what was happening, and he was going to do something about it. On September 14, he visited Ground Zero in New York City, where he climbed up a stack of debris from the fallen towers and turned to address the crowd, with this bullhorn in his hand.

Standing upon the debris of the World Trade Center, the President pledged that the voices calling for justice from across the country would be heard. As firefighter Bob Beckwith stood next to him listening, the President used this bullhorn to tell a group of first responders working in the debris, "I can hear you. The rest of the world hears you. And the people who knocked these buildings down will hear all of us soon." Responding to the President's words, rescue workers cheered and chanted "U.S.A.! U.S.A.! U.S.A.!"[8]

Today, the bullhorn is part of the George W. Bush Presidential Library and Museum's collection, which also contains a large archive of photographs and documents relating to September 11.

Barack Obama, 2009–2017: Pen Used to Sign the Affordable Care Act

One of the cornerstone achievements of Barack Obama's administration was the passage of the Affordable Care Act, colloquially known as "Obamacare," a sweeping health care reform bill that expanded coverage to millions of Americans. It had been a goal of the Democratic Party to redesign the American health care system since Harry Truman was president. Bill Clinton had come closest to making this happen, putting his wife, First Lady Hillary Clinton, in charge of a major policy initiative. The move did not sit well with many Americans, who questioned this unprecedented role for a first lady, who was expected to choose a signature issue that was a bit more palatable, such as Nancy Reagan's "Just Say No" antidrug campaign or Ladybird Johnson's focus on landscaping the nation's highways. Clinton was not able to get her plan on the Congress floor for a vote in 1994, and the issue was set aside until the next Democrat occupied the White House.[1]

On the campaign trail, Obama had promised to work on health care reform "by the end of his term," but after his election he decided it was best to tackle it right away, when his popularity was likely to be at its highest and the Democrats enjoyed strong majorities in both houses of Congress."[2] Although Democrats were united about health care reform, there was no consensus about what that might look like.

Some insisted that the federal government offer a "public-option" (that is, a government-run) coverage plan, and others urged that private coverage be extended to those who lacked it. More than three-fourths of Americans had

This was one of 22 pens that Barack Obama used to sign the Patient Protection and Affordable Care Act on March 23, 2010.
COURTESY BARACK OBAMA PRESIDENTIAL LIBRARY

private health insurance in some form, and despite the steeply rising costs of health care, many of them worried that changing the system might make their own situation worse, as well as adding to the federal budget deficit that the Recovery Act had already sent soaring above $1 trillion per year.[3]

Studying what had gone wrong with Clinton's plan, Obama sought to include legislators in the development of the plan, rather than keeping it secret. He also wanted to listen to the pharmaceutical and hospital industries who had lobbied heavily against Clinton's plan. To boost support, Obama made a televised address to Congress on September 9, 2009, where he said:

The plan I'm announcing tonight would meet three basic goals. It will provide more security and stability to those who have health insurance. It will provide insurance to those who don't. And it will slow the growth of health care costs for our families, our businesses, and our government. . . . Individuals will be required to carry basic health insurance—just as most states require you to carry auto insurance. Likewise, businesses will be required to either offer their workers health care, or chip in to help cover the costs of their workers.[4]

By the end of 2009, both houses of Congress had passed their own versions of Obama's plan. After some political wrangling to get the House to pass an unmodified version of the Senate's bill, Obama used this pen to sign the Patient Protection and Affordable Care Act on March 23, 2010. Most of the act has survived multiple attempts to repeal it since then.

When a president signs legislation, he uses several different pens to sign his name. According to CNN, "It's not clear which president started using multiple pens to sign single pieces of legislation. But historians do know the tradition stretches across decades. After the pens are used, they are typically handed out to those involved as a sort of historical artifact."[5] To sign the Affordable Care Act, Obama used a total of 22 pens. This one is from the collection of the Barack Obama Presidential Library.

Donald Trump, 2017–2021: MAGA Hat

Donald Trump was the most polarizing political figure in modern history. He is one of only five presidents to win the Electoral College vote but lose the popular vote. According to the Miller Center, Trump is also "the first president without previous service in either elective office or the military, as well as the oldest and among the richest to take office. He holds another distinction as well: Trump took office on January 20, 2017, with the lowest public approval ratings of any president since polling began after his campaign and transition were dogged with allegations of sexual improprieties and Russian meddling in the campaign on his behalf."[1]

The controversy started long before he took office. On June 16, 2015, Trump announced his candidacy for president at Trump Tower, where he also introduced the campaign slogan that would become a rallying cry: "Make America Great Again." Across the country, his campaign events were full of people wearing the now iconic red hats emblazoned with the phrase in white letters. In an interview with the BBC, market expert Ben Ostrower said, "I don't know if there has ever been a piece of fashion that inspires so much division and emotional turmoil."[2]

Some campaign slogans are so catchy and memorable, they remain familiar decades later, if only from vague recollections of high school history class. In 1840, William Henry Harrison used the slogan "Tippecanoe and Tyler Too." James K. Polk used "54-40 or Fight," referring to the geographic parallel of a border dispute with Great Britain in the Oregon Territory. In 1896, William McKinley used the alliterative phrase, "Patriotism, Protection, and Prosperity,"

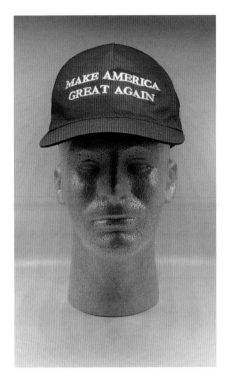

Donald Trump campaigned for president in 2016 with the slogan "Make America Great Again," which he had printed on hats that became a phenomenon on their own.
MCKINLEY PRESIDENTIAL LIBRARY & MUSEUM

which he followed with "Four More Years of a Full Dinner Pail" for his 1900 reelection campaign. In 1920, Warren G. Harding promised "A Return to Normalcy" after the tumultuous years of World War I. In 1928, Herbert Hoover pledged "A Chicken in Every Pot and a Car in Every Garage" for all Americans. In 1952, Dwight Eisenhower, who was the first to use television campaign ads, used the simple phrase "I Like Ike." In 2008, Barack Obama campaigned with the phrase, "Yes We Can."[3]

Trump repurposed Ronald Reagan's 1980 slogan, "Let's make America great again," which other candidates, including Bill Clinton, had also used in campaign speeches.[4] But he didn't just borrow it. He trademarked it back in November 2012 after Mitt Romney lost to Obama, according to Trump's 2016 campaign manager Corey Lewandowski. The hat as a vehicle for the phrase came from Trump himself, who liked to wear hats when he golfed.[5]

"Make America Great Again" was successful for many reasons. "It's emotional, it's simple and clear to understand, and it's participatory," said Ostrower. "However you feel about Donald Trump, he's a master salesman, and it's a credit to the MAGA hat that it is as divisive as it is. Arguably a lot of

Trump's tactics and Trumpism in the United States is about dividing people to sell a message. And the hat has been the symbol of achieving that." Those who chose to wear the hat have described it as a symbol of hope, pride, strength, or leadership. But for non-Trump supporters it became a symbol of division and even hatred. One unidentified African American woman told the BBC, "Bringing us back to a time when America was historically great was not great for people who looked like me."[6]

45

Joe Biden, 2021–:
COVID Vaccine Vial

Typically historians wait until approximately 20 years have passed in order to evaluate a historical event or time period, but the COVID-19 pandemic is likely to remain one of the biggest issues of Joe Biden's presidency. When he took office on January 20, 2021, his top two priorities were getting the pandemic under control and restarting the nation's economy. By the time he was inaugurated, over four hundred thousand Americans had already died.[1]

Biden got right to work. According to *Forbes*, on his first full day in office, he "signed 10 executive actions Thursday aimed at improving the government's response to the Covid-19 pandemic, jump-starting the president's ambitious plan to bring the current surge of cases under control and administer 100 million vaccinations in his first 100 days." The new orders included directing federal agencies to ramp up production of PPE, testing kits, and syringes; establishing a new pandemic testing board to increase testing capacity and a new COVID-19 Health Equity Task Force to identify and fix vaccination imbalances, particularly among minorities; enacting a mask mandate on interstate transportation and airports; increasing reimbursements from FEMA for virus-related expenses in schools; establishing a national security directive to work with global partners, such as the World Health Organization; and creating guidelines for schools to safely reopen. On the same day, Biden said, "We didn't get into this mess overnight and it is going to take months to get it turned around. But let me be equally clear, we will get through this, we will defeat this pandemic. . . . Help is on the way."[2]

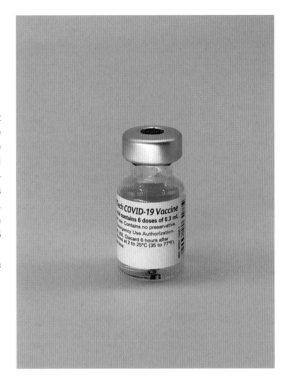

One of Joe Biden's biggest issues to tackle when he took office in 2021 was the COVID-19 pandemic. This vial contained enough Pfizer vaccine for six doses after it was diluted. The directions say, "Discard 6 hours after dilution when stored at 2 to 25° C (35 to 77° F)."

MCKINLEY PRESIDENTIAL LIBRARY & MUSEUM

The first group to receive the vaccination was those having the highest risk of hospitalization and death. Gradually, states released vaccine appointments to more adults, usually by age group and/or preexisting conditions. According to the CDC, by May 22, 2021, 57 percent of adults 18 and over in the United States had received at least one dose.[3] On May 10, 2021, the Food and Drug Administration approved the emergency use of the Pfizer vaccine for children aged 12 to 15. In a press release, Acting FDA Commissioner Janet Woodcock, MD, said, "Today's action allows for a younger population to be protected from COVID-19, bringing us closer to returning to a sense of normalcy and to ending the pandemic. Parents and guardians can rest assured that the agency undertook a rigorous and thorough review of all available data, as we have with all of our COVID-19 vaccine emergency use authorizations."[4] On September 22, 2021, Pfizer received authorization to provide booster shots to individuals over 65 or those who are at high risk.[5] On October 29, 2021, emergency authorization was given to Pfizer to begin administering a lower dose of its vaccine to children aged 5 to 11.[6]

In late summer 2021, Biden announced his "six-pronged, comprehensive national strategy that employs the same science-based approach that was used to successfully combat previous variants of COVID-19 earlier this year. This plan will ensure that we are using every available tool to combat COVID-19 and save even more lives in the months ahead, while also keeping schools open and safe, and protecting our economy from lockdowns and damage."[7] Outlined on the White House website, his strategy focused on vaccinating the unvaccinated, further protecting the vaccinated through booster shots, keeping schools safely open, increasing testing and maintaining mask requirements, protecting the country's economic recovery, and improving care for those who are diagnosed with COVID-19.

A significant portion of Americans refused to be vaccinated, which led to widespread hospitalizations during a surge of the Delta variant beginning in July 2021. Although breakthrough cases were possible for those who were vaccinated, the CDC reported that unvaccinated people were "10 times more likely to be hospitalized, and 11 times more likely to die of COVID-19."[8] In December 2021, exacerbated by a combination of COVID fatigue and holiday gatherings, the highly contagious and generally milder Omicron variant caused yet another surge of unvaccinated people being admitted to the hospital.[9]

This small glass vial represents the triumph of modern science over infectious disease. As the pandemic continues to unfold, the Biden administration's response to its challenges has helped to alter the course of the deadliest virus since the 1918 influenza pandemic.

Resolute Desk

The famous Resolute Desk, made from oak timbers from HMS *Resolute*, was a gift from Queen Victoria to Rutherford B. Hayes in 1880. A brass plaque on the desk preserves its history:

> HMS *Resolute*, forming part of the expedition sent in search of Sir John Franklin in 1852, was abandoned in Latitude 74° 41' N. Longitude 101° 22' W. on 15th May 1854. She was discovered and extricated in September 1855, in Latitude 67° N. by Captain Buddington of the United States Whaler *George Henry*. The ship was purchased, fitted out and sent to England, as a gift to Her Majesty Queen Victoria by the President and People of the United States, as a token of goodwill & friendship. This table was made from her timbers when she was broken up, and is presented by the Queen of Great Britain & Ireland, to the President of the United States, as a memorial of the courtesy and loving kindness which dictated the offer of the gift of the *Resolute*.[1]

Each president is permitted to furnish his office to his own tastes, choosing furniture and decorative arts from the White House collection. Every president since Hayes, with the exception of Lyndon B. Johnson, Richard Nixon, and Gerald Ford (1964–1977), have chosen to use the Resolute Desk, although some have preferred to use it in the private residence instead of the Oval Office. In 1962, the desk was made famous when the White House released an image of John F. Kennedy Jr., underneath it while his father worked. "John-John" was poking out from a hinged center panel that was added at the request of Franklin D. Roosevelt, who wanted to shield his leg braces from view. He died before the panel could be installed, but Harry Truman liked the eagle motif that was planned and had it installed when he took office in 1945. In the 1980s, Ronald Reagan requested that the desk be raised two inches to accommodate taller presidents.[2]

From 1880 to 1902, the Resolute Desk was used in the President's Office, which was located on the second floor of the residence. After Teddy Roosevelt's extensive renovations were completed in 1902, the official office was moved to the newly constructed West Wing, but the desk remained in the residence. After Harry Truman's renovations were completed in 1952, the desk was moved to the Broadcast Room, where Dwight D. Eisenhower used it to give radio and television broadcasts.

When the Kennedys arrived in the White House, Jackie Kennedy was appalled by its furnishings. Previous administrations had been permitted to sell items from the White House, and there was no preservation effort in place for

In 1880 Queen Victoria sent this desk, made from the timbers of HMS *Resolute*, as a gift to Rutherford B. Hayes. Almost every president since Hayes has used it.
WHITE HOUSE HISTORICAL ASSOCIATION

any of the historic treasures that were left. In 1961 she created the Fine Arts Committee, which would become the White House Historical Association. According to Sara Kettler, reporting on the website for the television series *Biography*, "She searched everywhere, from storage rooms to bathrooms, to unearth valuable items already in the White House. These efforts aided in the discovery of light rugs ordered by Theodore Roosevelt and French flatware from James Monroe's era. Century-old busts were found in a downstairs men's room. And she moved aside electric gear in a broadcast room to uncover the Resolute desk."[3] At Mrs. Kennedy's suggestion, John F. Kennedy became the first president to use it in the Oval Office, which was built in 1909 during Howard Taft's administration by architect Nathan C. Wyeth. Its iconic shape was inspired by the oval shape of the Blue Room.[4]

After Kennedy's assassination, Lyndon B. Johnson brought his own desk to the Oval Office, which was a mahogany pedestal partner's desk that he had used as a Texas senator.[5] From 1964 to 1965, the Resolute Desk was part of a traveling exhibition at the Kennedy Library. It was displayed in a Smithsonian exhibition from 1966 to 1977. When Jimmy Carter took office, he requested that the desk be returned to the White House.[6] The desk has come to symbolize the American presidency in the modern era.

Some museums, such as the Rutherford B. Hayes Presidential Library & Museums in Fremont, Ohio, have a replica of the Resolute Desk on display. In the President's Gallery at Hayes, visitors can sit behind it to see what it feels like to sit at such a historic desk. Replicas are available for purchase online, so anyone who can afford the price tag of up to $9,000, depending on the vendor, can have a piece of presidential history of their own.

47

Presidential Seal

For a televised speech or press conference, the president of the United States usually speaks from a lectern adorned with the official Presidential Seal of the United States. It is woven into the carpet in the Oval Office and painted on the side of Air Force One and the presidential limousine. It is used on all official White House correspondence. But it has not always appeared as it does today.

The presidential seal has its origins in the Great Seal of the United States, which was adopted by the Continental Congress in 1782 to generally represent the federal government. Three committee designs provided the inspiration for Continental Congress Secretary Charles Thomson's first design. In his original sketch, the stripes on the shield were arranged in a chevron design, and the eagle's wings were not spread out as far. William Barton suggested making the stripes vertical, as they appear in the modern design, and placing exactly 13 arrows in the eagle's talon, symbolic of the original 13 colonies.[1] When submitting his design to Congress, Thomson included an explanation of its symbolism:

> The Escutcheon is composed of the chief & pale, the two most honorable ordinaries. The Pieces, paly, represent the several states all joined in one solid compact entire, supporting a Chief, which unites the whole & represents Congress. The Motto alludes to this union. The pales in the arms are kept closely united by the Chief and the Chief depends on that union & the strength resulting from

it for its support, to denote the Confederacy of the United States of America & the preservation of their union through Congress.

The colours of the pales are those used in the flag of the United States of America; White signifies purity and innocence, Red, hardiness & valour, and Blue, the colour of the Chief signifies vigilance, perseverance & justice. The Olive branch and arrows denote the power of peace & war which is exclusively vested in Congress. The Constellation denotes a new State taking its place and rank among other sovereign powers. The Escutcheon is born on the breast of an American Eagle without any other supporters to denote that the United States of America ought to rely on their own Virtue.[2]

The presidential seal has become a recognizable symbol of the presidency, but its design was not standardized until Harry Truman's administration in 1945.
PUBLIC DOMAIN

The motto *e pluribus unum*, meaning "out of many, one," appeared in the original design, but was not always incorporated in subsequent designs.

Various versions of the seal have been used by presidential administrations over the years, but the design would not be standardized until Harry Truman signed Executive Order 9646 on October 25, 1945. Before that date, presidents could use whatever design they liked. James K. Polk used a version with an eagle on it for his letterhead, but there were only six arrows in its talon. In 1850 Millard Fillmore asked Maryland engraver Edward Stabler to design a seal for him. Fillmore sent him a very rough sketch, in which he wrote "eagle" in the center and "The Seal of the President of the US" around the perimeter. Stabler, who would go on to design seals for other federal offices and many states and cities, built upon the Continental Congress design, adding 30 stars to the foreground to symbolize the number of states and reducing the number of arrows in the eagle's talon to three. Abraham Lincoln used a similar design for his personal seal.[3]

Rutherford B. Hayes was the first president to use the seal for official White House invitations. Under his direction, the eagle's head was turned to face the talon with the arrows, rather than the olive branch. Truman's executive order officially fixed the eagle's head facing right, toward the olive branch, yet the myth persists that the eagle's head is turned to face the arrows during a time of war. In the novel *Deception Point*, author Dan Brown wrote that the Oval Office carpet is swapped out by the housekeeping staff at the White House in the dead of night after a declaration of war. Snopes.com addressed this urban legend, quoting White House Curator Bill Allman:

> There is just one Seal of the President at any given time, and it does not change according to whether or not the United States is at war. However, the Seal has undergone modifications over the years. President Truman modified the Seal in 1945, and the changes included turning the eagle's head to face its right as opposed to its left.
>
> A press release issued after the new design was approved said, "In the new Coat of Arms, Seal and Flag, the Eagle not only faces to its right—the direction of honor—but also toward the olive branches of peace which it holds in its right talon. Formerly the eagle faced toward the arrows in its left talon—arrows, symbolic of war."
>
> Although the eagle featured in the Presidential Seal has faced its right ever since, there are items in the White House collection that were made before 1945

that display the eagle facing its left (such as state services, furnishings, architectural elements, etc.).[4]

During an extensive renovation of the White House in 1902, Teddy Roosevelt asked sculptor Philip Martiny to incorporate Hayes's design, with the eagle facing the arrows, into a new presidential seal that was installed on the floor of the Entrance Hall.

The direction of the eagle's head was also an important element in presidential flag design, which incorporates the presidential seal. Without an official directive in place, each "official" flag design was unique. In 1882, the US Navy created the first presidential flag for Chester Arthur, which featured a version of the presidential seal with the eagle facing the olive branch on a dark navy blue background. In 1898 the US Army created its own flag, which used a different version of the presidential seal on a red background surrounded by 45 white stars and 4 additional stars in the corners. Again, the eagle was facing the olive branches. Woodrow Wilson issued Executive Order 2390 in 1916, which officially changed the flag design to the one used by the US Navy, using Martiny's presidential seal design. He also changed the eagle's head to face toward the arrows.[5]

Franklin Delano Roosevelt had begun discussions about changing the presidential seal at the end of World War II, but he would not live long enough to see his ideas implemented. Roosevelt, who was personally interested in symbolism and insignia, asked heraldry experts and military leaders for input on the new design. George Elsey, White House naval officer, and Arthur DuBois, chief of heraldry for the US Army, suggested turning the eagle's head and adding 48 stars, one for each state. After Roosevelt's death, Truman officially made the changes.[6] In his biography of Truman, historian David McCullough recounts Truman's reasoning:

> One morning, standing at his desk, he presented to the press a new presidential flag, telling Harry Vaughan to hold it high enough so that everyone could see, "This new flag faces the eagle toward the staff," Truman explained, "which is looking to the front all the time when you are on the march, and also has him looking at the olive branch for peace, instead of the arrows for war. . . ." Both the flag and presidential seal had been redesigned for the first time since the Wilson years, and Truman meant the shift in the eagle's gaze to be seen as symbolic of a nation both on the march and dedicated to peace.[7]

Snopes suggests that the proximity of these changes to war and peace could have fueled the myth of the eagle's head changing direction during wartime. Wilson changed it just before World War I, which could be misremembered as during the war, and Truman changed it back at the end of World War II.[8] The text of Truman's executive order, which is still in use today, reads:

By virtue of the authority vested in me as President of the United States, it is hereby ordered as follows:

The Coat of Arms of the President of the United States shall be of the following design:

SHIELD: Paleways of thirteen pieces Argent and Gules, a chief Azure; upon the breast of an American eagle displayed holding in his dexter talon an olive branch and in his sinister a bundle of thirteen arrows all Proper, and in his beak a white scroll inscribed "E PLURIBUS UNUM" Sable.

CREST: Behind and above the eagle a radiating glory Or, on which appears an arc of thirteen cloud puffs proper, and a constellation of thirteen mullets Argent.

The whole surrounded by white stars arranged in the form of an annulet with one point of each star outward on the imaginary radiating center lines, the number of stars conforming to the number of stars in the union of the Flag of the United States as established by the act of Congress approved April 4, 1818, 3 Stat. 415.

The Seal of the President of the United States shall consist of the Coat of Arms encircled by the words "Seal of the President of the United States."

Dwight D. Eisenhower subsequently changed the order in 1959 and 1960 when stars were added for Alaska and Hawaii, respectively.

From 1948 to 1952, Truman presided over a second major renovation of the White House. At that time, he ordered that the Martiny presidential seal in the floor of the Entrance Hall be relocated above the door of the Diplomatic Reception Room. Truman did not like the idea of White House visitors walking over the seal. He also placed a second presidential seal above the doorway of the Blue Room, "a symbolic reminder that the White House is both the people's house and the President's House."[9]

Use of the presidential seal is restricted to official use by the federal government only. Forbidden uses—and punishment for violators—are clearly spelled out in U.S. Code, Title 18, part I, chapter 33, paragraph 713: "Whoever knowingly displays any printed or other likeness of the great seal of the United States, or of the seals of the President or the Vice President of the United States . . . or any facsimile thereof, in, or in connection with, any advertisement, poster, circular, book, pamphlet, or other publication, public meeting, play, motion picture, telecast, or other production, or on any building, monument, or stationery, for the purpose of conveying, or in a manner reasonably calculated to convey, a false impression of sponsorship or approval by the Government of the United States or by any department, agency, or instrumentality thereof, shall be fined under this title or imprisoned not more than six months, or both."[10]

Official White House Portraits

An official White House portrait of each president and first lady has been part of the White House Historical Association's collection since 1965, when the organization acquired a portrait of Eleanor Roosevelt. Since then, it has been a "fundamental goal" to acquire portraits that are not represented in the collection, or to replace "earlier likenesses judged less than successful." Typically presidents and First Ladies select their artists just before leaving office, and the process usually takes a few years to complete. The WHHA negotiates a contract with the artist that includes a "confidentiality agreement so the artist's identity and details of the portrait are kept secret."[1] The former president and first lady are invited back for a formal presentation to the public when the portraits are completed. Jimmy Carter requested no ceremony, but every other president since Gerald Ford has participated in the unveiling. "These ceremonies are often bi-partisan events with warm greetings and collegial speeches exchanged by the president and his predecessor. The most recent unveiling took place in 2012 when President Barack Obama unveiled the White House portraits of former president George W. Bush and former First Lady Laura Bush."[2] The official portraits are hung in various spaces throughout the White House.

The most famous official portraits in the White House Historical Association collection are Gilbert Stuart's 1797 oil painting of George Washington and Aaron Shikler's 1970 oil painting of John F. Kennedy. Stuart's painting of Washington was made famous when First Lady Dolley Madison saved it from the British, who set fire to the White House during the War of 1812. It was the first painting to depict Washington as a statesman, rather than a military leader. According to the White House Historical Association, "Washington holds a sword in his left hand, alluding to his past military service, but appears in civilian clothes, emphasizing the fact that he had resigned his commission as a military leader. A book entitled *Constitution and Laws of the United States* leans against the table leg."[3]

By contrast, Kennedy's portrait depicts him with his arms folded, gazing downward, with his face obscured. Shikler worked directly with First Lady Jackie Kennedy several years after the president's death to create the image. In 1981 Shikler said, "The only stipulation she made was, 'I don't want him to look the way everybody else makes him look, with the bags under his eyes and that penetrating gaze. I'm tired of that image.'"[4] He was loosely inspired

This photograph of the Entrance Hall and the Grand Staircase was taken by Matthew D'Agostino on July 20, 2017, during the Donald Trump administration. Located on the State Floor of the White House, the Entrance Hall welcomes visitors arriving through the North Portico to the Executive Mansion. The Grand Staircase connects the Second Floor and family quarters of the White House with the State Floor and Entrance Hall below. During official occasions such as State Dinners, the president descends the staircase with honored guests while the United States Marine Band plays "Hail to the Chief." Visible are the official portraits of Harry Truman, Franklin D. Roosevelt, and Bill Clinton.

MATTHEW D'AGOSTINO FOR THE WHITE HOUSE HISTORICAL ASSOCIATION

by a photograph of Ted Kennedy at his brother's grave. The grim feeling of the painting was not supposed to symbolize his death. "I painted him with his head bowed, not because I think of him as a martyr, but because I wanted to show him as a president who was a thinker," Shikler said in 1971. "A thinking president is a rare thing. All presidential portraits have eyes that look right at you. I wanted to do something with more meaning. I hoped to show a courage that made him humble."[5] According to the White House Historical Association, "President Richard Nixon and First Lady Patricia Nixon hosted Jacqueline Kennedy and her children at the White House to see the portraits before they were publicly displayed."[6]

Outside of the White House, the Smithsonian's National Portrait Gallery has the largest collection of presidential portraits, which are usually commissioned by the president and first lady privately. Barack and Michelle Obama chose African American artists Kehinde Wiley and Amy Sherald, respectively, to paint their portraits, which made quite a splash for their departure from traditional style. The Obama portraits were financed by many private donors for the National Portrait Gallery.

49

Senate Ballot Box

According to Article II, Section 1 of the US Constitution, the Electoral College is charged with officially electing the president and vice president of the United States. Unlike most democracies around the world, the popular vote does not determine the winner. When Americans head to the polls on Election Day, they are essentially voting for the electors who will cast their votes in the Electoral College.

The creation of the Electoral College was a last-minute compromise during the Constitutional Convention. According to the United States House of Representatives, "Various methods for selecting the executive were offered, reviewed, and discarded during the Constitutional Convention: legislative; direct; gubernatorial; electoral; and lottery. A decision resulted only late in the Convention, when the Committee of Detail presented executive election by special electors selected by the state legislatures. This compromise preserved states' rights, increased the independence of the executive branch, and avoided popular election."[1]

Each state has as many electors as they have representatives in Congress, plus three from the District of Columbia, for a total of 538. The "magic number" to reach a majority is 270 electoral votes. According to the US Senate, "Certificates that attest to each state's balloting are brought from the Senate to a joint session of Congress in the House chamber for counting by the vice president."[2] This is what was happening on January 6, 2021, when the Capitol was overtaken by pro-Trump protestors.

This mahogany box held the certificates for the official tally on January 6, 1969, that confirmed the election of Richard Nixon as president. Mahogany boxes, similar in design to this box, have been used to carry the electoral ballots since 1877.
US SENATE COLLECTION

In most states, the electors vote for the winner of the popular vote within that state, however Maine and Nebraska use a "district system" in which "two at-large electors vote for the winner of the state's popular vote and one elector votes for the popular winner in each congressional district."[3] It is commonly understood that electors will vote as directed by the rules of their state, but they are not required to do so:

> Although it is not unconstitutional for electors to vote for someone other than those to whom they pledged their support, many states, as well as the District of Columbia, "bind" electors to their candidate using oaths and fines. During the nineteenth century, "faithless electors"—those who broke their pledge and voted for someone else—were rare, but not uncommon, particularly when it came to Vice Presidents. In the modern era, faithless electors are rarer still, and have never determined the outcome of a presidential election. There has been one faithless elector in each of the following elections: 1948, 1956, 1960, 1968,

1972, 1976, and 1988. A blank ballot was cast in 2000. In 2016, seven electors broke with their state on the presidential ballot and six did so on the vice presidential ballot.[4]

Over the years, there have been several controversial elections stemming from the Electoral College system. In 1876, Republican Rutherford B. Hayes of Ohio ran against Democrat Samuel Tilden of New York in a hotly contested campaign. According to the Hayes Presidential Library & Museums, "Tilden won the popular vote and led in the electoral college, but 19 votes from three Republican-controlled states (Louisiana, Florida, and South Carolina) remained disputed. Oregon's count was also challenged. Allegations of widespread voter fraud forced Congress to set up a special electoral commission to determine the winner, composed of fifteen congressmen and Supreme Court justices. The commission finally announced their decision only two days before the inauguration. The vote was 8–7 along party lines to award the disrupted Electoral College votes to Hayes, making him the winner."[5] In the 19th century, inaugurations were held on March 4, unless it fell on a Sunday, which it did in 1877. Fearing that Tilden supporters would attempt to install him during the technical one-day gap between presidencies, President Grant and Secretary of State Hamilton Fish suggested that Hayes should be sworn in on Saturday, March 3, in a private ceremony in the White House. The public ceremony was held as planned on March 5.[6]

In the modern era, two presidential candidates have won the popular vote, but lost in the Electoral College. In 2000, Al Gore received 543,895 more popular votes than George W. Bush, but he lost the Electoral College by 5 votes after the Supreme Court intervened and stopped a recount in Florida. In 2016, Hillary Clinton won 2,868,519 more popular votes than Donald Trump, but lost the electoral vote 232 to 306. These elections have renewed calls to abolish the Electoral College.

Supporters of the Electoral College credit it with preserving an important dimension of state-based federalism in our presidential elections and argue that it works to guarantee that our Presidents will have nationwide support. Critics argue under current circumstances that it actually consigns most states in the Union to "spectator" status in presidential elections and drags down voter turnout in these states, reduces the real field of play to fewer than a dozen "swing states," and dramatically polarizes the nation's politics while reducing voter turnout.[7]

In spite of the controversies surrounding it, the Electoral College remains intact as designated in the Constitution. Calls for change have gained momentum in recent years, but so far nothing has garnered enough support to challenge the system officially.

Air Force One

Technically, any airplane that flies with the president aboard is known as "Air Force One," but the term generally refers to "specific planes that are equipped to transport the Commander in Chief."[1] The Air Force established the unique call sign "Air Force One" in 1953 after a commercial flight with the number 8610 happened to fly into the same air space as President Eisenhower's plane with the call sign Air Force 8610.[2] According to the National Museum of the United States Air Force, "Today, this name refers to one of two highly customized Boeing 747-200B series aircraft, which carry the tail codes 28000 and 29000. The Air Force designation for the aircraft is VC-25A."[3] The Museum, located in Dayton, Ohio, is the official repository for Air Force aircraft that have been retired from the presidential aircraft fleet. The Presidential Gallery features 10 historical aircraft representing more than 70 years of dedicated presidential service.[4]

Teddy Roosevelt was the first president to ride in an airplane, but he did so after he left office. His distant cousin, Franklin D. Roosevelt, became the first sitting president to ride in an airplane: "In 1943, a Boeing 314 Clipper flying boat named the Dixie Clipper carried him 5,500 miles in three legs to attend the Casablanca Conference, where he met with Winston Churchill and Charles de Gaulle to discuss the next phase of World War II."[5] Travel by sea became increasingly dangerous during the war, with German submarines attacking both military and commercial ships, so transport by air was a safer option for the president.

The Douglas VC-54C Skymaster, known unofficially as the "Sacred Cow," was the first plane built with the intention of transporting the president:

> As the only VC-54C built, the aircraft was heavily modified on the assembly line. A C-54A fuselage was fitted with wings from a C-54B which offered greater fuel capacity. The unpressurized cabin included an executive conference room with a large desk and a rectangular bulletproof window. For additional comfort, a private lavatory was installed next to the president's seat, and a fold down bed was concealed behind the sofa. An electric refrigerator in the galley added an uncommon luxury for 1945. A battery-powered elevator was installed at the rear of the aircraft which allowed President Roosevelt to board the aircraft easily while in his wheelchair.[6]

Roosevelt only flew in the "Sacred Cow" once before his death, when he was flown to the Yalta Conference in February 1945. Harry Truman flew in it extensively. He was on board "Sacred Cow" when he signed the National Security Act of 1947, which established the US Air Force as its own branch of the military.

Visitors can climb aboard several aircraft that were used as Air Force One in the Presidential Gallery at the National Museum of the United States Air Force in Dayton, Ohio.
PHOTO BY KEN LAROCK FOR THE NATIONAL MUSEUM OF THE US AIR FORCE

The Douglas VC-118, which Truman named "The Independence" after his hometown, replaced the "Sacred Cow" in 1947.

> Different from the standard DC-6 configuration, The Independence included an aft stateroom for the president and a main cabin which seated 24 passengers or 12 "sleeper" berths. Other improvements included reversible-pitch propellers, weather radar, a radar altimeter, autopilot and other advanced navigation equipment. Water injection gave the engines more power at takeoff, and larger fuel tanks enabled it to fly nonstop to any location within the continental United States. The Independence had a unique, bright color scheme, recommended by the Douglas Aircraft Co., consisting of a stylized American eagle with the feathers carried down the fuselage to the vertical stabilizer.[7]

The first jet aircraft to serve as Air Force One was the Boeing VC-137C SAM 26000, a highly modified commercial aircraft that would serve eight US presidents from Kennedy to Clinton. First Lady Jackie Kennedy and industrial designer Raymond Loewy created the paint scheme that is so recognizable today. "In addition to the vibrant blue and white colors, the words 'United States of America' were emblazoned in tall letters along the fuselage and an American flag was placed on the tail. These distinctive markings reflect the stature of the Office of the President and serve as a highly visible symbol of American prestige."[8] The most famous scene on board this plane was the swearing-in ceremony of Lyndon B. Johnson after Kennedy's assassination, standing next to his widow, whose pink Chanel skirt was still covered in her husband's blood, just outside the camera's view. Visitors can climb aboard this aircraft at the National Museum of the United States Air Force and stand in the exact spot where this historic event took place.

The Air Force ordered two new Boeing 747 aircraft, with tail codes 28000 and 29000, during Ronald Reagan's administration, but they were not ready until after George H. W. Bush took office. These planes are still in use today. (New aircraft have been ordered, but they may not be delivered until 2025.) The current planes are well equipped to serve the president: "Capable of refueling midair, Air Force One has unlimited range and can carry the President wherever he or she needs to travel. The onboard electronics are hardened to protect against an electromagnetic pulse, and Air Force One is equipped with advanced secure communications equipment, allowing the aircraft to function as a mobile command center in the event of an attack on the United States."[9] On the morning of September 11, 2001, George W. Bush boarded

SAM 28000 and took off from Sarasota-Bradenton International Airport in Florida, initially circling over the Gulf of Mexico while the president was briefed on the situation and decisions were made on what to do next.

The modern Air Force One is also equipped with a medical suite that can function as an operating room for the doctor who is always assigned to the plane. There is enough galley space to feed up to one hundred people at a time. The 4,000 square feet on three different levels includes a large presidential suite with an office, conference room, and private lavatory, as well as quarters for those who accompany the president when he travels.[10]

Notes

CHAPTER 1. GEORGE WASHINGTON, 1789–1797: DENTURES

1. "The Trouble with Teeth," Mount Vernon, accessed March 18, 2021, https://www
.mountvernon.org/george-washington/health/washingtons-teeth/.

2. "False Teeth," Mount Vernon, accessed March 18, 2021, https://www.mount
vernon.org/library/digitalhistory/digital-encyclopedia/article/false-teeth/.

3. "False Teeth."

4. "How George Washington's Teeth—from Animals and Maybe Slaves—Became
an American Legend," Stat News, accessed March 29, 2021, https://www.statnews
.com/2017/07/03/george-washington-teeth/.

5. "False Teeth."

6. "George Washington and Teeth from Enslaved People," Mount Vernon, accessed
March 18, 2021, https://www.mountvernon.org/george-washington/health
/washingtons-teeth/george-washington-and-slave-teeth/.

7. "The Trouble with Teeth."

8. *All About History Book of US Presidents* (London: Imagine Publishing, 2016),
12–14.

9. "Did George Washington Really Free Mount Vernon's Enslaved Workers?" History Channel, accessed March 18, 2021, https://www.history.com/news/did -george-washington-really-free-mount-vernons-slaves.

10. "George Washington and Slavery," Mount Vernon, accessed March 18, 2021, https://www.mountvernon.org/library/digitalhistory/digital-encyclopedia/article /george-washington-and-slavery/.

CHAPTER 2. JOHN ADAMS, 1797–1801: LAW DESK

1. *All About History Book of US Presidents* (London: Imagine Publishing, 2016), 23.

2. C. James Taylor, "John Adams: Campaigns and Elections," Miller Center, University of Virginia, accessed March 21, 2021, https://millercenter.org/president /adams/campaigns-and-elections.

3. Kelly Cobble, email to author, March 23, 2021.

4. Ed Finkel, "John Adams Gets His Day: The First Lawyer-President Set a Standard for Representing Unpopular Causes," *ABA Journal*, May 1, 2001, accessed April 7, 2022, https://www.abajournal.com/magazine/article/john_adams_gets_his_day.

5. James West Davidson, *Nation of Nations* (New York: McGraw-Hill, 1994), 290.

6. Taylor, "John Adams: Campaigns and Elections."

7. The Naturalization, Alien Enemies, and Sedition Acts had been passed by Congress and signed by Adams, which greatly expanded the president's powers. The Naturalization Act lengthened the residency period to become a US citizen from 5 years to 14 years. Since immigrants tended to support Democratic Republican candidates, the act was designed to benefit Adams and the Federalists. The Alien Enemies Act authorized Adams to arrest and deport aliens whom he deemed were a threat to national security. The Sedition Act "established heavy fines and even imprisonment for writing, speaking, or publishing anything of 'a false, scandalous and malicious' nature against the government. Davidson, *Nation of Nations*, 293; and C. James Taylor, "John Adams: Domestic Affairs," The Miller Center, University of Virginia, accessed March 21, 2021, https://millercenter.org/president/adams /domestic-affairs.

8. Taylor, "John Adams: Campaigns and Elections."

9. Taylor, "John Adams: Campaigns and Elections."

10. C. James Taylor, "John Adams: Life after the Presidency," The Miller Center, University of Virginia, accessed March 21, 2021, https://millercenter.org/president/adams/life-after-the-presidency.

CHAPTER 3. THOMAS JEFFERSON, 1801–1809: GREAT CLOCK AT MONTICELLO

1. "Great Clock," Monticello, accessed March 11, 2021, https://www.monticello.org/site/research-and-collections/great-clock.

2. Susan Stein, *The Worlds of Thomas Jefferson at Monticello* (Charlottesville, VA: Thomas Jefferson Memorial Foundation, 1993), 376–77.

3. "Great Clock."

4. "Great Clock."

5. "Great Clock."

6. *All About History Book of US Presidents* (London: Imagine Publishing, 2016), 27.

7. "Jefferson's Attitudes toward Slavery," Monticello, accessed March 11, 2021, https://www.monticello.org/thomas-jefferson/jefferson-slavery/jefferson-s-attitudes-toward-slavery/.

8. "The Life of Sally Hemings," Monticello, accessed March 11, 2021, https://www.monticello.org/sallyhemings/.

9. "Jefferson's Attitudes toward Slavery."

CHAPTER 4. JAMES MADISON, 1809–1817: WALKING STICK

1. Hilarie M. Hicks, email to author February 10, 2021.

2. *All About History Book of US Presidents* (London: Imagine Publishing, 2016), 28.

3. Hilarie M. Hicks and Elizabeth Ladner, "Briefing Paper: The Madison-Jefferson Relationship," MRD-S 47664 (Orange, VA: Montpelier Foundation, March 13, 2017), 1.

4. Hicks and Ladner, "Briefing Paper," 2.

5. *All About History Book of US Presidents*, 29.

6. *All About History Book of US Presidents*, 29.

7. Hilarie M. Hicks, "'When I Had the Happiness of Possessing You at Monticello': A Timeline of James Madison's Visits to Thomas Jefferson's Monticello," research report, MRD-S 47466 (Orange, VA: Montpelier Foundation, June 19, 2017, updated May 29, 2018), 2.

8. Hilarie M. Hicks, "'As Your Better Judgment May Chuse': Looking for Jefferson's Influence on Madison's Montpelier," research report, MRD-S 43741 (Orange, VA: Montpelier Foundation, September 2, 2015), 2.

9. Hicks and Ladner, "Briefing Paper: The Madison-Jefferson Relationship," 2.

10. Hicks, "'As Your Better Judgment May Chuse,'" 3–4.

11. Hicks, email.

CHAPTER 5. JAMES MONROE, 1817–1825: DESK

1. Jarod Kearney, assistant director and curator of the James Monroe Museum and Memorial Library, personal correspondence with the author, August 31, 2021.

2. "Monroe Doctrine (1823)," Our Documents, accessed September 16, 2021, https://www.ourdocuments.gov/doc.php?flash=false&doc=23.

3. "Monroe Doctrine," Office of the Historian, State Department, accessed September 16, 2021, https://history.state.gov/milestones/1801-1829/monroe.

4. "Monroe Doctrine (1823)."

5. "Monroe Doctrine (1823)."

6. Daniel Preston, "James Monroe: Foreign Affairs," The Miller Center, University of Virginia, accessed September 16, 2021, https://millercenter.org/president/monroe/foreign-affairs.

7. "Objects," James Monroe Museum, accessed April 6, 2022, https://james monroemuseum.umw.edu/collections/objects/.

CHAPTER 6. JOHN QUINCY ADAMS, 1825–1829: PERSONAL LIBRARY

1. All About History Book of US Presidents (London: Imagine Publishing, 2016), 32.

2. Kelly Cobble, Adams National Historical Park, correspondence with the author, April 9, 2021.

3. Cobble, correspondence with the author, April 7, 2021.

4. Margaret A. Hogan, "John Quincy Adams: Life before the Presidency," The Miller Center, University of Virginia, accessed March 26, 2021, https://millercenter.org /president/jqadams/life-before-the-presidency.

5. Margaret A. Hogan, "John Quincy Adams Overview," The Miller Center, University of Virginia, accessed March 26, 2021, https://millercenter.org/president/jqadams.

6. Cobble, correspondence with the author, April 7, 2021.

7. Sara Georgini, "John Quincy Adams Kept a Diary and Didn't Skimp on the Details," *Smithsonian Magazine*, July 11, 2017, accessed April 7, 2022, https://www .smithsonianmag.com/history/john-quincy-adams-kept-diary-and-didnt-skimp -details-180964011/.

8. "Foundation Document Overview," Adams National Historical Park, accessed May 28, 2021, http://npshistory.com/publications/foundation-documents/adam -fd-overview.pdf.

CHAPTER 7. ANDREW JACKSON, 1829–1837: DECAPITATED FIGUREHEAD

1. "U.S.S. *Constitution*," National Park Service, accessed March 31, 2021, https:// www.nps.gov/parkhistory/online_books/founders/sitec22.htm.

2. "Off with His Head," USS *Constitution* Museum, accessed March 31, 2021, https://ussconstitutionmuseum.org/2015/07/02/off-with-his-head/.

3. Anonymous letter to the editor, *Vermont Republican and American Journal*, April 3, 1834.

4. Sam Roberts, "President's Features Reunited after 176 Years," *New York Times*, April 4, 2010.

5. "Description of the Figure Head," *Western Carolinian*, May 24, 1834.

6. "Off with His Head."

7. "Two seventy-fours" refers to the ships USS *Independence* and USS *Columbus*. A "seventy four" was a type of two-decked ship that usually carried 74 guns.

8. The Figure Head, *Fayetteville Weekly Observer*, July 15, 1834.

9. Madeleine Hazelwood, "The Beheading of President Andrew Jackson," Museum of the City of New York, accessed March 31, 2021, https://www.mcny.org/story /beheading-president-andrew-jackson.

10. Roberts, "President's Features Reunited after 176 Years."

CHAPTER 8. MARTIN VAN BUREN, 1837–1841: DESK

1. Joel Silbey, "Martin Van Buren: Life in Brief," The Miller Center, University of Virginia, accessed May 26, 2021, https://millercenter.org/president/vanburen/life-in-brief.

2. Joel Silbey, "Martin Van Buren: Domestic Affairs," The Miller Center, University of Virginia, accessed May 27, 2021, https://millercenter.org/president/vanburen/domestic-affairs; *All About History Book of US Presidents* (London: Imagine Publishing, 2016), 39.

3. Joel Silbey, "Martin Van Buren: Life after the Presidency," The Miller Center, University of Virginia, accessed May 27, 202, https://millercenter.org/president/vanburen/life-after-the-presidency.

4. "Martin Van Buren National Historic Site, Lindenwald, New York," National Park Service, accessed May 27, 2021, https://www.nps.gov/nr/travel/presidents/van_buren_lindenwald.html.

CHAPTER 9. WILLIAM HENRY HARRISON, 1841: FLAG REMNANT

1. *All About History Book of US Presidents* (London: Imagine Publishing, 2016), 41.

2. William Freehling, "William Harrison: Life before the Presidency," The Miller Center, University of Virginia, accessed May 27, 2021, https://millercenter.org/president/harrison/life-before-the-presidency.

3. Freehling, "William Harrison: Life before the Presidency."

4. Roger Hardig, correspondence with the author, November 6, 2020.

5. Freehling, "William Harrison: Life before the Presidency."

6. William Freehling, "William Harrison: Campaigns and Elections," The Miller Center, University of Virginia, accessed May 27, 2021, https://millercenter.org/president/harrison/campaigns-and-elections.

7. Jane McHugh and Philip A. Mackowiak, "What Really Killed William Henry Harrison?," *New York Times*, March 31, 2014, accessed April 6, 2022, https://www.nytimes.com/2014/04/01/science/what-really-killed-william-henry-harrison.html.

CHAPTER 10. JOHN TYLER, 1841–1845: PIANO

1. Amy Tikkanen, "The Surprisingly Disorderly History of the U.S. Presidential Succession Order," *Britannica*, accessed May 28, 2021, https://www.britannica.com /story/the-surprisingly-disorderly-history-of-the-us-presidential-succession-order.

2. Jonathan L. Stoltz, "Many American Presidents Have Had Hidden Musical Abilities," *Virginia Gazette*, April 27, 2021, accessed April 6, 2022, https://www .dailypress.com/virginiagazette/opinion/va-vg-ed-oped-presidential-music-0428 -20210427-uwoqea6hojfs3d7lcxsj2npfty-story.html.

CHAPTER 11. JAMES K. POLK, 1845–1849: TABLE

1. "Manifest Destiny," The History Channel, accessed May 28, 2021, https://www .history.com/topics/westward-expansion/manifest-destiny.

2. Candice Candeto, President James K. Polk Home & Museum, correspondence with the author, February 5, 2021.

3. Candeto, correspondence with the author.

4. "Manifest Destiny," The History Channel.

5. *Frank Freidel and Hugh Sidey,* "James K. Polk," The White House Historical Association, accessed May 28, 2021, https://www.whitehouse.gov/about-the-white -house/presidents/james-k-polk/.

6. "Attack of the Killer White House—Did the White House Itself Lead to the Death of Several 19th Century Presidents?," *History Is Now Magazine*, September 20, 2015, accessed April 6, 2022, http://www.historyisnowmagazine.com/blog/2015/9/12 /attack-of-the-killer-white-house-did-the-white-house-itself-lead-to-the-death-of -several-19th-century-presidents#.Yk30hfXMK3I=.

CHAPTER 12. ZACHARY TAYLOR, 1849–1850: CHAIR

1. *All About History Book of US Presidents* (London: Imagine Publishing, 2016), 46.

2. *Frank Freidel and Hugh Sidey,* "Zachary Taylor," The White House Historical Association, accessed May 28, 2021, https://www.whitehouse.gov/about-the-white -house/presidents/zachary-taylor/.

3. Object Record 1951.33, Kentucky Historical Society, accessed May 28, 2021, https://kyhistory.pastperfectonline.com/webobject/9FEF902B-1D82-434E-9F2C -280121800300.

4. Patricia Poore, "Decorative Motifs II," *Arts & Crafts Homes,* August 13, 2020, accessed April 7, 2022, https://artsandcraftshomes.com/interiors/decorative-motifs-ii.

5. Michael Holt, "Zachary Taylor: Life before the Presidency," The Miller Center, University of Virginia, accessed May 28, 2021, https://millercenter.org/president/taylor/life-before-the-presidency.

6. Michael Holt, "Zachary Taylor: Campaigns and Elections," The Miller Center, University of Virginia, accessed May 28, 2021, https://millercenter.org/president/taylor/life-before-the-presidency.

7. Michael Holt, "Zachary Taylor: Domestic Affairs," The Miller Center, University of Virginia, accessed June 1, 2021, https://millercenter.org/president/taylor/life-before-the-presidency.

8. "Attack of the Killer White House—Did the White House Itself Lead to the Death of Several 19th Century Presidents?," *History Is Now Magazine,* September 20, 2015, accessed April 6, 2022, http://www.historyisnowmagazine.com/blog/2015/9/12/attack-of-the-killer-white-house-did-the-white-house-itself-lead-to-the-death-of-several-19th-century-presidents#.Yk30hfXMK3I=.

CHAPTER 13. MILLARD FILLMORE, 1850–1853: ENGRAVING OF DEBATE

1. Michael Holt, "Millard Fillmore: Domestic Affairs," The Miller Center, University of Virginia, accessed June 1, 2021, https://millercenter.org/president/fillmore/domestic-affairs.

2. "The United States Senate, A.D. 1850," United States Senate, accessed April 7, 2022, https://www.senate.gov/art-artifacts/historical-images/prints-engravings/38_00029.htm.

3. Rachelle Moyer Frances, correspondence with the author, January 26, 2021.

4. "Compromise of 1850," The History Channel, accessed June 1, 2021, https://www.history.com/topics/abolitionist-movement/compromise-of-1850.

5. "Compromise of 1850."

6. Holt, "Millard Fillmore: Domestic Affairs."

7. Holt, "Millard Fillmore: Domestic Affairs."

CHAPTER 14. FRANKLIN PIERCE, 1853–1857: KANSAS-NEBRASKA ACT

1. Jean H. Baker, "Franklin Pierce: Life in Brief," The Miller Center, University of Virginia, accessed September 1, 2021, https://millercenter.org/president/pierce/life -in-brief.

2. "Jean H. Baker, Franklin Pierce: Campaigns and Elections," The Miller Center, University of Virginia, accessed September 2, 2021, https://millercenter.org /president/pierce/life-in-brief.

3. Baker, "Franklin Pierce: Campaigns and Elections."

4. Jean H. Baker, "Franklin Pierce: Domestic Affairs," The Miller Center, University of Virginia, accessed September 1, 2021, https://millercenter.org/president/pierce /domestic-affairs.

5. Baker, "Franklin Pierce: Domestic Affairs."

6. Jean H. Baker, "Franklin Pierce: Impact and Legacy," The Miller Center, University of Virginia, accessed September 17, 2021, https://millercenter.org /president/pierce/impact-and-legacy.

7. Jay Tolson, "Worst Presidents: Franklin Pierce (1853–1857)," *US News and World Report*, February 16, 2007, accessed September 17, 2021, https://www.usnews.com /news/special-reports/the-worst-presidents/articles/2014/12/17/worst-presidents -franklin-pierce-1853-1857.

8. Jean H. Baker, "Franklin Pierce: Life after the Presidency," The Miller Center, University of Virginia, accessed September 2, 2021, https://millercenter.org /president/pierce/life-after-the-presidency.

CHAPTER 15. JAMES BUCHANAN, 1857–1861: LAW BOOKS

1. Patrick Clarke, personal correspondence with the author, April 28, 2021.

2. William Cooper, "James Buchanan: Life in Brief," The Miller Center, University of Virginia, accessed June 1, 2021, https://millercenter.org/president/buchanan/life-in -brief.

3. W. U. Hensel, "James Buchanan as a Lawyer," speech delivered March 28, 1912, University of Pennsylvania Carey Law School, accessed September 2, 2021, https:// scholarship.law.upenn.edu/cgi/viewcontent.cgi?article=7259&context=penn_law _review.

4. Hensel, "James Buchanan as a Lawyer."

5. Hensel, "James Buchanan as a Lawyer."

6. William Cooper, "James Buchanan: Life before the Presidency," The Miller Center, University of Virginia, accessed September 5, 2021, https://millercenter.org/president/buchanan/life-before-the-presidency.

7. Cooper, "James Buchanan: Life before the Presidency."

8. William Cooper, "James Buchanan: Campaigns and Elections," The Miller Center, University of Virginia, accessed September 5, 2021, https://millercenter.org/president/buchanan/campaigns-and-elections.

9. William Cooper, "James Buchanan: Domestic Affairs," The Miller Center, University of Virginia, accessed September 5, 2021, https://millercenter.org/president/buchanan/domestic-affairs.

10. Cooper, "James Buchanan: Domestic Affairs."

11. Hensel, "James Buchanan as a Lawyer."

CHAPTER 16. ABRAHAM LINCOLN, 1861–1865: CHAIR FROM FORD'S THEATRE

1. James West Davidson, *Nation of Nations* (New York: McGraw-Hill, 1994), 556; *All About History Book of US Presidents* (London: Imagine Publishing, 2016), 57.

2. "Whispering Gallery," Abraham Lincoln Presidential Library and Museum, accessed on March 20, 2021, https://www.lincolnlibraryandmuseum.com/whispering-gallery.

3. "United States Colored Troops: The Role of African Americans in the US Army," American Battlefield Trust, accessed March 29, 2021, https://www.battlefields.org/learn/topics/united-states-colored-troops.

4. "Slavery, Civil War, and Democracy: What Did Lincoln Believe?," Constitutional Rights Foundation, accessed on March 20, 2021, https://www.crf-usa.org/bill-of-rights-in-action/bria-22-4-b-slavery-civil-war-and-democracy-what-did-lincoln-believe.html; "Lincoln's Second Inaugural Address," National Park Service, accessed on April 7, 2022, https://www.nps.gov/linc/learn/historyculture/lincoln-second-inaugural.htm.

5. "Rocking Chair Used by Abraham Lincoln at Ford's Theatre the Night of His Assassination, April 14, 1865," Henry Ford Museum, accessed on March 20, 2021,

https://www.thehenryford.org/collections-and-research/digital-collections
/artifact/73805/#slide=gs-3272071.

6. "Rocking Chair Used by Abraham Lincoln at Ford's Theatre."

CHAPTER 17. ANDREW JOHNSON, 1865–1869: IMPEACHMENT NOTE

1. Elizabeth R. Varon, "Andrew Johnson: Life in Brief," The Miller Center, University of Virginia, accessed September 5, 2021, https://millercenter.org/president/johnson /life-in-brief.

2. David O. Stewart, "The Assassination of Abraham Lincoln: The Family Plot to Kill Lincoln," *Smithsonian Magazine*, accessed September 5, 2021. https://www .smithsonianmag.com/history/the-family-plot-to-kill-lincoln-2093807/.

3. "Black Codes," The History Channel, accessed September 5, 2021, https://www .history.com/topics/black-history/black-codes.

4. Varon, "Andrew Johnson: Life in Brief."

5. "Resolution of Impeachment of President Andrew Johnson," National Archives, accessed September 5, 2021, https://catalog.archives.gov/id/2127356.

6. "Impeachment Trial of Andrew Johnson, 1868," United States Senate, accessed April 7, 2022, https://www.senate.gov/about/powers-procedures/impeachment /impeachment-johnson.htm.

7. Elizabeth R. Varon, "Andrew Johnson: Domestic Affairs," The Miller Center, University of Virginia, accessed September 5, 2021, https://millercenter.org /president/johnson/domestic-affairs.

CHAPTER 18. ULYSSES S. GRANT, 1869–1877: INKWELL

1. Joan Waugh, "Ulysses S. Grant: Life in Brief," The Miller Center, University of Virginia, accessed September 6, 2021, https://millercenter.org/president/grant/life -in-brief.

2. Melissa Trombley-Prosch, "Some Notes on Grant's White House Years," unpublished document, shared with the author, February 8, 2021.

3. Sotheby's Auction Catalog, Item #166 in Sotheby's January 18 and 19, 2001, Important Americana Auction.

4. Jackson Arn, "Why Democrats Are Donkeys and Republicans Are Elephants," CNN, accessed September 6, 2021, https://www.cnn.com/style/article/why -democrats-are-donkeys-republicans-are-elephants-artsy/index.html.

5. Arn, "Why Democrats Are Donkeys and Republicans Are Elephants."

CHAPTER 19. RUTHERFORD B. HAYES, 1877–1881: MORGAN SILVER DOLLAR

1. Robert D. Johnston, "Rutherford B. Hayes: Domestic Affairs," The Miller Center, University of Virginia, accessed September 6, 2021, https://millercenter.org /president/hayes/domestic-affairs.

2. "Financial Panic of 1873," United States Treasury, accessed September 6, 2021, https://home.treasury.gov/about/history/freedmans-bank-building/financial -panic-of-1873.

3. Johnston, "Rutherford B. Hayes: Domestic Affairs."

4. "The Heyday of the Gold Standard 1820–1930." World Gold Council, accessed September 6, 2021, https://www.gold.org/sites/default/files/documents/1875jan14 .pdf.

5. Johnston, "Rutherford B. Hayes: Domestic Affairs."

6. "Morgan Silver Dollar," Rutherford B. Hayes Presidential Library & Museums, accessed September 6, 2021, https://www.rbhayes.org/estate/morgan-silver-dollar/.

7. "Morgan Silver Dollar."

8. "Morgan Silver Dollar."

CHAPTER 20. JAMES A. GARFIELD, 1881: INAUGURAL ADDRESS

1. "James Garfield Inaugural Ball 1881," White House Historical Association, accessed September 6, 2021, https://www.whitehousehistory.org/photos/james -garfield-inaugural-ball-1881.

2. "President Garfield and the Smithsonian," Smithsonian, accessed September 6, 2021, https://si-siris.blogspot.com/2016/02/president-garfield-and-smithsonian.html.

3. "President Garfield and the Smithsonian."

4. The American Presidency Project, "James Garfield Inaugural Address," https:// www.presidency.ucsb.edu/documents/inaugural-address-39, accessed May 25, 2022.

5. "Justus Doenecke, "James A. Garfield: Impact and Legacy," The Miller Center, University of Virginia, accessed September 6, 2021, https://millercenter.org /president/garfield/impact-and-legacy.

CHAPTER 21. CHESTER ARTHUR, 1881–1885: TIFFANY SCREEN

1. Justus Doenecke, "Chester Arthur: Domestic Affairs," The Miller Center, University of Virginia, accessed September 6, 2021, https://millercenter.org /president/arthur/domestic-affairs.

2. Doenecke, "Chester Arthur: Domestic Affairs."

3. "An Essay on *The Grand Illumination* by Peter Wadell," White House Historical Association, accessed September 6, 2021, https://www.whitehousehistory.org/the -grand-illumination-sunset-of-the-gaslight-age-1891-by-peter-waddell.

4. "An Essay on *The Grand Illumination* by Peter Wadell."

5. "An Essay on *The Grand Illumination* by Peter Wadell."

6. Milrose Consultants, "A History of White House Renovations," accessed September 6, 2021, https://www.milrose.com/insights/a-history-of-white-house -renovations.

7. Facebook post, White House Historical Association, March 25, 2015.

CHAPTER 22. GROVER CLEVELAND, 1885–1889 AND 1893–1897: NAVAL REVIEW RIBBON

1. Sharon Farrell, personal correspondence with the author, March 29, 2021.

2. Farrell, personal correspondence with the author, September 10, 2021.

3. Joseph C. Mosier, "The Naval Rendezvous of 1893," USS *San Francisco*, accessed September 7, 2021, https://usssanfrancisco.org/the-naval-rendezvous-of-1893-by -joseph-c-mosier/.

4. Mosier, "The Naval Rendezvous of 1893."

5. Mosier, "The Naval Rendezvous of 1893."

6. Hilary A. Herbert, "The Lesson of the Naval Review," *North American Review* 156, no. 439 (June 1893), accessed September 7, 2021, https://www.jstor.org/stable /pdf/25103145.pdf.

7. "Grover Cleveland: First Annual Message (second term)," The American Presidency Project, University of California at Santa Barbara, accessed September 7, 2021, https://www.presidency.ucsb.edu/documents/first-annual-message-second-term.

CHAPTER 23. BENJAMIN HARRISON, 1889–1893: *JUDGE* CARTOON

1. Heather Cox Richardson, "When Adding New States Helped the Republicans," *Atlantic*, September 19, 2019, accessed September 7, 2021, https://www.theatlantic.com/ideas/archive/2019/09/when-adding-new-states-helped-republicans/598243/.

2. Allan B. Spetter, "Benjamin Harrison: The American Franchise," The Miller Center, University of Virginia, accessed September 7, 2021, https://millercenter.org/president/bharrison/the-american-franchise.

3. Richardson, "When Adding New States Helped the Republicans."

4. Merrill Fabry, "Now You Know: Why Are There Two Dakotas?," *Time*, July 14, 2016, accessed September 7, 2021, https://time.com/4377423/dakota-north-south-history-two/.

5. Richardson, "When Adding New States Helped the Republicans."

6. "The Admissions Clause," National Constitution Center, accessed September 8, 2021, https://constitutioncenter.org/interactive-constitution/interpretation/article-iv/clauses/46.

7. "The Admissions Clause."

CHAPTER 24. WILLIAM MCKINLEY, 1897–1901: MCKINLEY NATIONAL MEMORIAL COLLECTION BANK

1. James West Davidson, *Nation of Nations* (New York: McGraw-Hill, 1994), 821.

2. Christopher Kenney, "The Assassination of President William McKinley: A Catalyst for Change in Protecting the President," *White House History Quarterly*, White House Historical Association, no. 57, 8.

3. Kenney, "The Assassination of President William McKinley, 8.

4. Kenney, "The Assassination of President William McKinley," 11–14.

5. Christopher Kenney, *The McKinley Monument: A Tribute to a Fallen President* (Mount Pleasant, SC: Arcadia, 2006), 31.

6. Kenney, "The Assassination of President William McKinley," 14.

7. Kenney, "The Assassination of President William McKinley," 14.

8. Kenney, "The Assassination of President William McKinley," 17.

9. Kenney, "The Assassination of President William McKinley," 17.

CHAPTER 25. THEODORE ROOSEVELT, 1901–1909: PAGE FROM SPEECH

1. Sidney Milkis, "Theodore Roosevelt: Campaigns and Elections," The Miller Center, University of Virginia, accessed September 8, 2021, https://millercenter.org/president/roosevelt/campaigns-and-elections.

2. "When Teddy Roosevelt Was Shot in 1912, a Speech May Have Saved His Life," The History Channel, accessed September 8, 2021, https://www.history.com/news/shot-in-the-chest-100-years-ago-teddy-roosevelt-kept-on-talking.

3. Patricia O'Toole, "The Speech That Saved Teddy Roosevelt's Life," *Smithsonian*, accessed September 8, 2021, https://www.smithsonianmag.com/history/the-speech-that-saved-teddy-roosevelts-life-83479091/.

4. O'Toole, "The Speech That Saved Teddy Roosevelt's Life."

5. "When Teddy Roosevelt Was Shot in 1912, a Speech May Have Saved His Life."

6. Milkis, "Theodore Roosevelt: Campaigns and Elections."

7. O'Toole, "The Speech That Saved Teddy Roosevelt's Life."

CHAPTER 26. WILLIAM HOWARD TAFT, 1909–1913: BIBLE

1. "Taft Gained Peaks in Unusual Career," *New York Times*, March 9, 1930, accessed September 8, 2021, http://www.arlingtoncemetery.net/whtaft.htm.

2. "Taft Gained Peaks in Unusual Career."

3. "William Howard Taft's Truly Historic 'Double-Double,'" National Constitution Center, accessed September 8, 2021, https://constitutioncenter.org/blog/william-howard-tafts-truly-historic-double-double.

4. Erick Trickey, "Chief Justice, Not President, Was William Howard Taft's Dream Job," *Smithsonian*, accessed September 8, 2021, https://www.smithsonianmag.com/history/chief-justice-not-president-was-william-howard-tafts-dream-job-180961279/.

CHAPTER 27. WOODROW WILSON, 1913–1921: 1919 PIERCE-ARROW

1. Andrew Phillips, curator and director of museum operations, Woodrow Wilson Presidential Library, personal correspondence with the author, November 6, 2020.

2. Saladin Ambar, "Woodrow Wilson: Foreign Affairs," The Miller Center, University of Virginia, accessed September 9, 2021, https://millercenter.org/president/wilson/foreign-affairs.

3. "The Paris Peace Conference and the Treaty of Versailles," Office of the Historian, US State Department, accessed September 9, 2021, https://history.state.gov/milestones/1914-1920/paris-peace.

4. Phillips, personal correspondence with the author.

5. Phillips, personal correspondence with the author.

6. Phillips, personal correspondence with the author.

7. Phillips, personal correspondence with the author.

CHAPTER 28. WARREN G. HARDING, 1921–1923: SKELETON KEY

1. Sherry Hall, quoted in Edward Loomis, foreword, in Sherry Hall, *Warren G. Harding and the* Marion Daily Star: *How Newspapering Shaped a President* (Mt. Pleasant, SC: Arcadia, 2014), 9.

2. Sherry Hall, *Warren G. Harding and the* Marion Daily Star: *How Newspapering Shaped a President* (Mt. Pleasant, SC: Arcadia, 2014), 11.

3. Hall, *Warren G. Harding and the* Marion Daily Star, 17.

4. Hall, *Warren G. Harding and the* Marion Daily Star, 88.

5. Hall, *Warren G. Harding and the* Marion Daily Star, 102.

6. Hall, *Warren G. Harding and the* Marion Daily Star, 113.

CHAPTER 29. CALVIN COOLIDGE, 1923–1929: PAINTING OF INAUGURATION

1. William W. Jenney, Regional Historic Site administrator, Vermont Division for Historic Preservation, President Calvin Coolidge State Historic Site, personal correspondence with the author, June 4, 2021.

2. Jenney, personal correspondence with the author.

3. Jenney, personal correspondence with the author.

CHAPTER 30. HERBERT HOOVER, 1929–1933: HUMIDOR

1. Matthew Schaefer, "Hoover Ball and Wellness in the White House," *White House History Quarterly*, no. 55, The Presidents and Sports, 46.

2. Schaefer, "Hoover Ball and Wellness in the White House," 46.

3. Schaefer, "Hoover Ball and Wellness in the White House," 51.

4. Schaefer, "Hoover Ball and Wellness in the White House," 46.

5. "Hoover Tosses Ball in Daily Dozen," *News-Journal*, Mansfield, Ohio, March 25, 1929, 1.

6. Schaefer, "Hoover Ball and Wellness in the White House," 46.

7. *All About History Book of US Presidents* (London: Imagine Publishing, 2016), 93.

8. James West Davidson, *Nation of Nations* (New York: McGraw-Hill, 1994), 978.

9. Davidson, *Nation of Nations*, 974–75.

CHAPTER 31. FRANKLIN D. ROOSEVELT, 1933–1945: FIRESIDE CHAT MICROPHONE

1. James West Davidson, *Nation of Nations* (New York: McGraw-Hill, 1994), 982.

2. "The Development of Radio," *The American Experience*, PBS, accessed March 2, 2021, https://www.pbs.org/wgbh/americanexperience/features/rescue-development-radio/.

3. "Radio," *Encyclopedia Britannica*, accessed March 2, 2021, https://www.britannica.com/topic/radio.

4. Richard Kurin, *The Smithsonian's History of America in 101 Objects* (New York: The Penguin Press, 2013), 401–5.

5. Franklin Delano Roosevelt, "On the Bank Crisis," Franklin D. Roosevelt Presidential Library and Museum, March 12, 1933, accessed March 2, 2021, http://docs.fdrlibrary.marist.edu/031233.html.

6. "The Fireside Chats," History Channel, accessed March 2, 2021, https://www.history.com/topics/great-depression/fireside-chats.

7. Kurin, *The Smithsonian's History of America in 101 Objects*, 404.

8. "The Fireside Chats."

9. Christopher H. Sterling, "The Fireside Chats," Library of Congress, accessed March 2, 2021, https://www.loc.gov/static/programs/national-recording -preservation-board/documents/FiresideChats.pdf.

10. Sterling, "The Fireside Chats."

11. Kurin, *The Smithsonian's History of America in 101 Objects*, 404.

12. "The Fireside Chats."

CHAPTER 32. HARRY S. TRUMAN, 1945–1953: "THE BUCK STOPS HERE" DESK SIGN

1. "'The Buck Stops Here' Desk Sign," Harry S. Truman Presidential Library, accessed September 9, 2021, https://www.trumanlibrary.gov/education/trivia/buck -stops-here-sign.

2. "'The Buck Stops Here' Desk Sign."

3. Alonzo L. Hamby, "Harry S. Truman: Life in Brief," The Miller Center, University of Virginia, accessed September 9, 2021, https://millercenter.org/president/truman /life-in-brief.

4. Hamby, "Harry S. Truman: Life in Brief."

5. "'The Buck Stops Here' Desk Sign."

CHAPTER 33. DWIGHT D. EISENHOWER, 1953–1961: GLOBE

1. Robert Peary is officially credited as the first person to reach the North Pole, but Matt Henson, who was part of the exploration party, maintained that he was actually there first. "Matthew Henson: The Pioneering African-American Arctic Adventurer," *The Guardian*, accessed September 10, 2021, https://www.theguardian.com/travel /2020/may/24/matthew-henson-arctic-explorer-first-man-to-north-pole.

2. Chester J. Pach Jr., "Dwight D. Eisenhower: Campaigns and Elections," The Miller Center, University of Virginia, accessed September 10, 2021, https://millercenter.org /president/eisenhower/campaigns-and-elections.

3. Chester J. Pach Jr., "Dwight D. Eisenhower: Foreign Affairs," The Miller Center, University of Virginia, accessed September 10, 2021, https://millercenter.org /president/eisenhower/foreign-affairs.

4. Chester J. Pach Jr., "Dwight D. Eisenhower: Impact and Legacy," The Miller Center, University of Virginia, accessed September 10, 2021, https://millercenter.org /president/eisenhower/impact-and-legacy.

5. "Eisenhower Quotes," Dwight D. Eisenhower Presidential Library, Museum and Boyhood Home, accessed September 10, 2021, https://www.eisenhowerlibrary.gov /eisenhowers/quotes.

CHAPTER 34. JOHN F. KENNEDY, 1961–1963: PT 109 COCONUT HUSK PAPERWEIGHT

1. Janice Hodson, supervisory museum curator, John F. Kennedy Presidential Library and Museum, personal correspondence with the author, April 29, 2021.

2. "John F. Kennedy and PT 109," John F. Kennedy Presidential Library and Museum, accessed September 10, 2021, https://www.jfklibrary.org/learn/about-jfk /jfk-in-history/john-f-kennedy-and-pt-109.

3. "John F. Kennedy and PT 109."

4. "John F. Kennedy and PT 109."

5. Hodson, personal correspondence with the author.

6. Hodson, personal correspondence with the author.

CHAPTER 35. LYNDON B. JOHNSON, 1963–1969: DESK BLOTTER

1. Kent Germany, "Lyndon B. Johnson: Domestic Affairs," The Miller Center, University of Virginia, accessed September 13, 2021, https://millercenter.org /president/lbjohnson/domestic-affairs.

2. Germany, "Lyndon B. Johnson: Domestic Affairs."

3. Germany, "Lyndon B. Johnson: Domestic Affairs."

4. Kent Germany, "Lyndon B. Johnson: Impact and Legacy," The Miller Center, University of Virginia, accessed September 13, 2021, https://millercenter.org /president/lbjohnson/impact-and-legacy.

5. Germany, "Lyndon B. Johnson: Impact and Legacy."

CHAPTER 36. RICHARD NIXON, 1969–1974: EASY CHAIR

1. Evan Thomas, "The Complexity of Being Richard Nixon," *The Atlantic*, accessed April 7, 2022, https://www.theatlantic.com/politics/archive/2015/06/the-complexity-of-being-richard-nixon/394547/.

2. Tom Wicker, "Richard M. Nixon," in *Character Above All: Ten Presidents from FDR to George Bush* (New York: Simon & Schuster, 1997), excerpt available at PBS New Hour, accessed September 13, 2021, https://www.pbs.org/newshour/spc/character/essays/nixon.html.

3. Christine Mickey, acting supervisory museum curator of the Richard Nixon Presidential Library and Museum, Correspondence with Terri Garner, director, William J. Clinton Presidential Library, acting director, Office of Presidential Libraries, forwarded to the author on February 9, 2021.

4. H. R. Haldeman Diaries Collection, January 20, 1970, Richard Nixon Presidential Library and Museum, accessed September 13, 2021, https://www.nixonlibrary.gov/sites/default/files/virtuallibrary/documents/haldeman-diaries/37-hrhd-journal-vol04-19700121.pdf.

5. H. R. Haldeman Diaries Collection, October 12, 1972, Richard Nixon Presidential Library and Museum, accessed September 13, 2021, https://www.nixonlibrary.gov/sites/default/files/virtuallibrary/documents/haldeman-diaries/37-hrhd-audiocassette-ac25b-19721012-pa.pdf.

6. H. R. Haldeman Diaries Collection, November 1, 1972, Richard Nixon Presidential Library and Museum, accessed September 13, 2021, https://www.nixonlibrary.gov/sites/default/files/virtuallibrary/documents/haldeman-diaries/37-hrhd-audiocassette-ac26a-19721101-pa.pdf.

7. "The Museum," Richard Nixon Presidential Library and Museum, accessed September 13, 2021, https://www.nixonlibrary.gov/museum.

CHAPTER 37. GERALD FORD, 1974–1977: STATUETTE OF ELEPHANT AND DONKEY

1. "Gerald R. Ford," The White House, accessed September 13, 2021, https://www.whitehouse.gov/about-the-white-house/presidents/gerald-r-ford/.

2. John Robert Greene, "Gerald Ford: Life in Brief," The Miller Center, University of Virginia, accessed September 13, 2021, https://millercenter.org/president/ford/life-in-brief.

3. Donald Holloway, personal correspondence with the author, February 9, 2021.

4. Greene, "Gerald Ford: Life in Brief."

5. Greene, "Gerald Ford: Life in Brief."

CHAPTER 38. JIMMY CARTER, 1977–1981: HUNGARIAN CROWN

1. Robert A. Strong, "Jimmy Carter: Life in Brief," The Miller Center, University of Virginia, accessed September 14, 2021, https://millercenter.org/president/carter/life-in-brief.

2. Brittany Parris, personal correspondence with the author, November 12, 2021.

3. "Museum Items: The Crown of St. Stephen," Jimmy Carter Presidential Library and Museum, accessed December 2, 2021, https://www.jimmycarterlibrary.gov/museum/museum_items.

4. Memo to President Carter from Hamilton Jordan, undated, accessed December 2, 2021, https://www.jimmycarterlibrary.gov/digital_library/cos/142099/34/cos_142099_34b_05-Hungary.pdf.

5. Letter to President Carter from Jeane Dixon, November 7, 1977, accessed December 2, 2021, https://www.jimmycarterlibrary.gov/digital_library/sso/148878/50/SSO_148878_050_01.pdf.

6. "Museum Items: The Crown of St. Stephen."

7. "Museum Items: The Crown of St. Stephen."

8. Robert A. Strong, "Jimmy Carter: Domestic Affairs," The Miller Center, University of Virginia, accessed September 14, 2021, https://millercenter.org/president/carter/domestic-affairs.

CHAPTER 39. RONALD REAGAN, 1981–1989: PIECE OF THE BERLIN WALL

1. "President Reagan Challenges Gorbachev to 'Tear down This wall,'" The History Channel, accessed September 15, 2021, https://www.history.com/this-day-in-history/reagan-challenges-gorbachev-to-tear-down-the-berlin-wall.

2. Peter Robinson, "Tear Down This Wall: How Top Advisers Opposed Reagan's Challenge to Gorbachev—But Lost," National Archives, Summer 2007, accessed September 15, 2021, https://www.archives.gov/publications/prologue/2007/summer/berlin.html.

3. Robinson, "Tear Down This Wall."

4. Robinson, "Tear Down This Wall."

5. "Inside the Reagan Library—The Berlin Wall and South Lawn," Ronald Reagan Presidential Library and Museum, accessed September 15, 2021, https://www .reaganfoundation.org/programs-events/webcasts-and-podcasts/podcasts/videocasts /inside-the-reagan-library-the-berlin-wall-and-south-lawn/.

CHAPTER 40. GEORGE H. W. BUSH, 1989–1993: LETTER TO FAMILY

1. The Persian Gulf War would later become known as the First Gulf War.

2. Jay Patton, personal communication with the author, February 5, 2021.

3. "Persian Gulf War," The History Channel, accessed September 15, 2021, https:// www.history.com/topics/middle-east/persian-gulf-war.

4. "Persian Gulf War."

CHAPTER 41. BILL CLINTON, 1993–2001: SAXOPHONE

1. Deborah Check Reeves, "The 'Number One Bill Clinton' Tenor Saxophone," The Metropolitan Museum of Art, accessed September 15, 2021, https://www .metmuseum.org/blogs/of-note/2015/bill-clinton-saxophone.

2. "Today in TV History: Bill Clinton and His Sax Visit Arsenio," TV Insider, accessed September 15, 2021, https://www.tvinsider.com/2979/rerun-bill-clinton -on-arsenio-hall/.

3. "Today in TV History: Bill Clinton and His Sax Visit Arsenio."

4. "Today in TV History: Bill Clinton and His Sax Visit Arsenio."

5. "Jazz Museum Gets Clinton Saxophone," *Chicago Tribune*, December 21, 2007, accessed September 15, 2021, https://www.chicagotribune.com/news/ct-xpm-2007 -12-21-0712201212-story.html.

6. Reeves, "The 'Number One Bill Clinton' Tenor Saxophone."

CHAPTER 42. GEORGE W. BUSH, 2001–2009: BULLHORN

1. Ann Compton, "Covering the President from the Last Plane in Flight: September 11, 2001," *White House History*, no. 62, Fall 2021.

2. Compton, "Covering the President from the Last Plane in Flight: September 11, 2001."

3. Remarks on the Terrorist Attack on New York City's World Trade Center in Sarasota, Florida, George W. Bush, National Archives, September 11, 2001, accessed September 16, 2021, https://catalog.archives.gov/id/77828633.

4. Compton, "Covering the President from the Last Plane in Flight: September 11, 2001."

5. George W. Bush, Remarks on the Terrorist Attacks at Barksdale Air Force Base, Louisiana, National Archives, September 11, 2001, accessed September 16, 2021, https://catalog.archives.gov/id/77828635.

6. Aaron Sanderford, "When Bush Came to Nebraska: 9/11 through the Eyes of Those at Offutt That Day," KMTV *News Now Omaha*, September 10, 2021, accessed September 30, 2021.

7. Compton, "Covering the President from the Last Plane in Flight: September 11, 2001."

8. "Featured Artifact," George W. Bush Presidential Library and Museum, accessed September 16, 2021, https://georgewbushlibrary.smu.edu/en/Visit/Exhibits/Featured -Artifact.

CHAPTER 43. BARACK OBAMA, 2009–2017: PEN USED TO SIGN THE AFFORDABLE CARE ACT

1. Amy Goldstein, "How the Demise of Her Health-Care Plan Led to the Politician Clinton Is Today," *Washington Post*, August 25, 2016, accessed September 16, 2021, https://www.washingtonpost.com/politics/after-health-care-missteps-a-chastened -hillary-clinton-emerged/2016/08/25/2d200cb4-64b4-11e6-be4e-23fc4d4d12b4 _story.html.

2. Michael Nelson, "Barack Obama: Domestic Affairs," The Miller Center, University of Virginia, accessed September 16, 2021, https://millercenter.org/president/obama /domestic-affairs.

3. Nelson, "Barack Obama: Domestic Affairs."

4. Nelson, "Barack Obama: Domestic Affairs."

5. Leah Asmelash, "Why Do Presidents Use So Many Pens to Sign Documents—and What Happens to Them?," CNN, January 22, 2021, accessed September 16, 2021, https://www.cnn.com/2021/01/22/us/pens-biden-executive-order-trnd/index.html.

CHAPTER 44. DONALD TRUMP, 2017–2021: MAGA HAT

1. Jackie Calmes, "Donald Trump: Campaigns and Elections," The Miller Center, University of Virginia, accessed September 16, 2021, https://millercenter.org /president/trump/campaigns-and-elections.

2. What Does This Hat Mean to Americans?," BBC, June 19, 2019, accessed September 16, 2021, https://www.bbc.com/news/av/world-us-canada-48665944.

3. Indulekha Aravind, "Slogans That Have Rent the Air in US Presidential Campaigns," *Economic Times*, November 2, 2020, accessed September 16, 2021, https://economictimes.indiatimes.com/news/international/world-news/slogans -that-have-rent-the-air-in-us-presidential-campaigns/all-the-presidents-slogans /slideshow/78998049.cms.

4. "Presidential Campaign Slogans," Presidents USA, accessed September 16, 2021, https://www.presidentsusa.net/campaignslogans.html; and Aravind, "Slogans That Have Rent the Air in US Presidential Campaign."

5. "What Does This Hat Mean to Americans?"

6. "What Does This Hat Mean to Americans?"

CHAPTER 45. JOE BIDEN, 2021–: COVID VACCINE VIAL

1. "Joe Biden: Domestic Affairs," The Miller Center, University of Virginia, accessed September 16, 2021, https://millercenter.org/joe-biden-domestic-affairs.

2. Alison Durkee, "Here's What Biden Did about Covid-19 on His First Full Day as President," *Forbes*, January 21, 2021, accessed September 16, 2021, https://www .forbes.com/sites/alisondurkee/2021/01/21/biden-covid-19-response-executive -orders-on-first-full-day-as-president/?sh=482397f816b3.

3. "COVID-19 Vaccination Coverage among Adults—United States, December 14, 2020–May 22, 2021," Centers for Disease Control and Prevention, June 25, 2021, accessed September 16, 2021, https://www.cdc.gov/mmwr/volumes/70/wr/mm7025 e1.htm.

4. "Coronavirus (COVID-19) Update: FDA Authorizes Pfizer-BioNTech COVID-19 Vaccine for Emergency Use in Adolescents in Another Important Action in Fight against Pandemic," Food and Drug Administration, May 10, 2021, accessed September 16, 2021, https://www.fda.gov/news-events/press-announcements /coronavirus-covid-19-update-fda-authorizes-pfizer-biontech-covid-19-vaccine -emergency-use.

5. FDA Press Release, "FDA Authorizes Booster Dose of Pfizer-BioNTech COVID-19 Vaccine for Certain Populations," September 22, 2021, accessed April 7, 2022, https://www.fda.gov/news-events/press-announcements/fda-authorizes -booster-dose-pfizer-biontech-covid-19-vaccine-certain-populations.

6. FDA Press Release, "FDA Authorizes Pfizer-BioNTech COVID-19 Vaccine for Emergency Use in Children 5 through 11 Years of Age," October 29, 2021, accessed April 7, 2022, https://www.fda.gov/news-events/press-announcements/fda -authorizes-pfizer-biontech-covid-19-vaccine-emergency-use-children-5-through -11-years-age.

7. "Path Out of the Pandemic: President Biden's COVID-19 Action Plan," The White House, accessed September 16, 2021, https://www.whitehouse.gov/covidplan/.

8. "Unvaccinated People Were 11 Times More Likely to Die of COVID-19, CDC Report Finds," Lena H. Sun and Joel Achenbach, *Washington Post*, September 10, 2021, accessed September 16, 2021, https://www.washingtonpost.com/health /2021/09/10/moderna-most-effective-covid-vaccine-studies/.

9. Centers for Disease Control, "COVID-19–Associated Hospitalizations among Adults during SARS-CoV-2 Delta and Omicron Variant Predominance, by Race/ Ethnicity and Vaccination Status—COVID-NET, 14 States, July 2021–January 2022," March 25, 2022, accessed April 7, 2022, https://www.cdc.gov/mmwr/volumes/71/wr /mm7112e2.htm.

CHAPTER 46. RESOLUTE DESK

1. "Treasures of the White House: The 'Resolute' Desk," White House Historical Association, accessed September 7, 2021, https://www.whitehousehistory.org/photos /treasures-of-the-white-house-resolute-desk.

2. "Resolute Desk," The White House Museum, accessed September 7, 2021, http:// www.whitehousemuseum.org/west-wing/resolute-desk.htm.

3. Sara Kettler, "How Jacqueline Kennedy Transformed the White House and Left a Lasting Legacy," *Biography*, April 23, 2019, accessed September 28, 2021, https://www.biography.com/news/jacqueline-kennedy-white-house-restoration.

4. "Why Is the Oval Office Oval?," White House Historical Association, accessed September 7, 2021, https://www.whitehousehistory.org/questions/why-is-the-oval-office-oval.

5. Facebook post, White House Historical Association, January 27, 2021.

6. "Treasures of the White House: The 'Resolute' Desk."

CHAPTER 47. PRESIDENTIAL SEAL

1. Matthew Costello, "A Brief History of the Presidential Seal," White House Historical Association, https://www.whitehousehistory.org/a-brief-history-of-the-presidential-seal, accessed March 28, 2021.

2. Jimmy Stamp, "Who Designed the Seal of the President of the United States?," *Smithsonian Magazine*, https://www.smithsonianmag.com/arts-culture/who-designed-the-seal-of-the-president-of-the-united-states-5162560/, accessed March 28, 2021.

3. Stamp, "Who Designed the Seal of the President of the United States?"

4. David Mikkelson, "Does the U.S. Presidential Seal Change in Wartime?," Snopes, https://www.snopes.com/fact-check/presidential-seal-change-war/, accessed March 28, 2021.

5. Costello, "A Brief History of the Presidential Seal."

6. Costello, "A Brief History of the Presidential Seal."

7. David McCollough, *Truman* (New York: Simon & Schuster, 1992), 569.

8. Mikkelson, "Does the U.S. Presidential Seal Change in Wartime?"

9. Costello, "A Brief History of the Presidential Seal."

10. "Chapter 33—Emblems, Insignia, and Names." US Code. https://uscode.house.gov/view.xhtml?path=/prelim@title18/part1/chapter33&edition=prelim.

CHAPTER 48. OFFICIAL WHITE HOUSE PORTRAITS

1. "White House Portrait Ceremony May Be the Latest Casualty of the Political Divide," NBC News, accessed September 16, 2021, https://www.nbcnews.com/news/amp/ncna1209676.

2. Official White House Portraits, White House Historical Association, accessed September 15, 2021, https://www.whitehousehistory.org/press-room/press-back grounders/official-white-house-portraits.

3. "George Washington," White House Historical Association, accessed September 14, 2021, https://www.whitehousehistory.org/photos/george-washington-by-gilbert -stuart.

4. Caroline Hallemann, "The Story Behind JFK's Official White House Portrait," *Town & Country*, accessed September 14, 2021, https://www.townandcountrymag .com/society/politics/a18197437/president-kennedy-official-portrait/.

5. Hallemann, "The Story Behind JFK's Official White House Portrait."

6. "Official White House Portraits," White House Historical Association, accessed September 14, 2021, https://www.whitehousehistory.org/press-room/press-back grounders/official-white-house-portraits.

CHAPTER 49. SENATE BALLOT BOX

1. "Electoral College and Indecisive Elections," United States House of Representatives, accessed September 7, 2021, https://history.house.gov/Institution /Origins-Development/Electoral-College/.

2. "Ballot Box, Electoral College," United States Senate, accessed September 7, 2021, https://www.senate.gov/art-artifacts/decorative-art/other/79_00001.htm.

3. "Electoral College Fast Facts," United States House of Representatives, accessed September 7, 2021, https://history.house.gov/Institution/Electoral-College/Electoral -College/.

4. "Electoral College Fast Facts."

5. "The Disputed Election of 1876," Rutherford B. Hayes Presidential Library & Museums, accessed September 7, 2021, https://www.rbhayes.org/hayes/disputed -election-of-1876/.

6. "Frequently Asked Questions on the 1876 Election," Rutherford B. Hayes Presidential Library & Museums, accessed September 7, 2021, https://www.rbhayes .org/hayes/frequently-asked-questions-on-the-1876-election/.

7. "Article II, Section 1, Clauses 2 and 3," National Constitution Center, accessed September 7, 2021, https://constitutioncenter.org/interactive-constitution/inter pretation/article-ii/clauses/350.

CHAPTER 50. AIR FORCE ONE

1. "Air Force One: The President's Office in the Sky," The White House, accessed September 14, 2021, https://www.whitehouse.gov/about-the-white-house/the -grounds/air-force-one/.

2. Jay Bennet, "A Visual History of Air Force One: Presidential Air Travel over the Past 100 Years," *Popular Mechanics*, accessed September 14, 2021, https://www .popularmechanics.com/flight/a20916/visual-history-air-force-one/.

3. "Air Force One: The President's Office in the Sky."

4. Rob Bardua, chief, Public Affairs Division, National Museum of the US Air Force, personal correspondence with the author, September 14, 2021.

5. Bennet, "A Visual History of Air Force One."

6. "Douglas VC-54C 'Sacred Cow' Fact Sheet," National Museum of the United States Air Force, accessed September 14, 2021, https://www.nationalmuseum.af.mil /Visit/Museum-Exhibits/Fact-Sheets/Display/Article/195813/douglas-vc-54c-sacred -cow/.

7. "Douglas VC-118 'The Independence' Fact Sheet," National Museum of the United States Air Force, accessed September 14, 2021, https://www.nationalmuseum .af.mil/Visit/Museum-Exhibits/Fact-Sheets/Display/Article/195804/douglas-vc-118 -independence/.

8. "Boeing VC-137C SAM 26000 Fact Sheet," National Museum of the United States Air Force, accessed September 14, 2021, https://www.nationalmuseum .af.mil/Visit/Museum-Exhibits/Fact-Sheets/Display/Article/195807/boeing-vc -137c-sam-26000/.

9. "Air Force One: The President's Office in the Sky."

10. "Air Force One: The President's Office in the Sky."

Index

About the Author

Kimberly A. Kenney became curator of the McKinley Presidential Library & Museum in October 2001 and was promoted to executive director in 2019. She graduated summa cum laude from Wells College in Aurora, New York, with a major in American history and minor in creative writing. She earned her master of arts degree in history museum studies at the Cooperstown Graduate Program.

Exploring the American Presidency through 50 Historic Treasures is Kim's ninth book. Her other books include *Interpreting Anniversaries and Milestones at Museums and Historic Sites*, *Stark County Food: From Early Farming to Modern Meals* (with coauthor Barb Abbott of Canton Food Tours), and *Murder in Stark County*. Her work has been published in the *Public Historian*, the journal of the National Council for Public History; *White House History*, the journal of the White House Historical Association; the *Repository*; the *Boston Globe*; *Aviation History*; and the literary magazine *Mused*. Kim has appeared on *The Daily Show*, *First Ladies: Influence and Images*, and *Mysteries at the Museum*. Her program "The 1918 Influenza Pandemic" was featured on C-SPAN's series American History TV.